LEGALIZE THIS!

VERSO

PRACTICAL ETHICS

GENERAL EDITOR: COLIN MCGINN

The purpose of this series is to provide clear analyses of topical and important moral issues written by experts in an accessible style suitable for both the student and the general public.

Douglas N. Husak: *Legalize This! The Case for Decriminalizing Drugs*
Mark Rowlands: *Animals Like Us*

LEGALIZE THIS!

THE CASE FOR DECRIMINALIZING DRUGS

DOUGLAS N. HUSAK

VERSO

London • New York

First published by Verso 2002
© Douglas Husak
All rights reserved
The moral rights of the author have been asserted

1 3 5 7 9 10 8 6 4 2

Verso
UK: 6 Meard Street, London W1F 0EG
USA: 180 Varick Street, New York, NY 10014–4606
www.versobooks.com

Verso is the imprint of New Left Books

ISBN 1–85984–663–7
ISBN 1–85984–320–4 (pbk)

British Library Cataloguing in Publication Data
A catalogue record for this book is available from the British Library

Library of Congress Cataloging-in-Publication Data
A catalog record for this book is available from the Library of Congress

Typeset in Garamond
Printed and bound in the USA by R.R. Donnelley & Sons

CONTENTS

ACKNOWLEDGEMENTS

Earlier versions of this manuscript were read by Colin McGinn, George Galfalvi, and Allan Horwitz. Each offered valuable assistance in helping me to improve it.

I owe a special debt to the dozens of students in my classes and seminars who constantly challenged me to refine and clarify my views about drug decriminalization and the arguments on its behalf.

EDITOR'S INTRODUCTION

Colin McGinn

The issue of drugs and the criminal law tends to be clouded by images of needle-inserting junkies, homeless crack addicts, violent street-corner dealers. Surely we don't want to encourage such things, and isn't the law relating to drugs precisely designed to minimize these kinds of problems? Without it wouldn't we be flooded with more of the same? Drug use has many evil consequences, and the laws against drugs are there to keep these under some sort of control. That, at any rate, is the conventional wisdom.

But suppose we look at a different problem: fatty foods. People overeat and grow obese, their health suffers, they may die prematurely. None of this is good. Statistics show that obesity and its associated ailments are a very large public health issue, especially in the United States. Overweight people find it extremely hard to reduce their weight to healthy proportions, despite the manifest risks to their well-being. They keep eating those fatty foods, so temptingly displayed in the supermarkets and advertised on television – they can't say No. They cannot properly control the quantity and quality of their diet. And this is not a joke – obesity is a major cause of emotional suffering, ill health, and death. What should be done about it? What about *criminalizing* it? That's right, put people in jail who consume lots of fatty foods. Outlaw the sale of such foods. Limit by law the amount of food a person can order in a restaurant or have in their fridge. This would – it might be argued – reduce or eliminate the problem, especially if the punishments were harsh enough. Soon we will have a nation of slim, healthy, happy people! People are motivated by fear, and if we scare people with the threat of jail time they will shape up and moderate their food intake. Of course, this is ultimately for their own good: think of the 300-pound diabetic at death's door – don't we want to save him from himself? If we had punished his youthful gluttony, he would have been saved. The introduction of laws against fatty foods is simply a rational response to a manifest social problem – tough love backed by the judicial system. This is crazy. But *why* is it crazy? Not because obesity is not a serious health problem. It is crazy, first, to think that this could really solve the problem: for surely the new laws will be broken, a black market will emerge, criminal activity relating to fatty foods will flourish. If you can't get your corn chips at the supermarket, you will buy them from your dealer on the corner. It is easy to see how this will generate an entire culture of law-breaking, violence, and packed jails. But second, and more important, such laws would be totally *unjust*: eating a bag of nachos is *not* like robbing a bank, or hitting someone, or even speeding. To incarcerate someone because of the food they eat is the wrong *kind* of response to their problem; criminal punishment is not an appropriate way to deal with eating disorders. Chiefly, this is because obesity does not harm others, nor is it intended to. The same point could be made about sex: there are many harmful effects of sex, particularly the contraction of serious diseases like AIDS. Would it be a good idea to criminalize sex in order to contain these problems? That way – it may be argued – we really will put a stop to the AIDS epidemic, since people will not engage in sex if they face serious jail time if caught. But, again, this is crazy. People will have sex anyway; the problem is not large enough to warrant such extreme infringements of liberty; the negative consequences would be huge (no more families); and it would be highly unjust to put people away simply for having sex – say, a married couple neither of whom has any sexually transmitted disease. The weight of the law should not be invoked in this way to handle a public health issue; instead, education and medical care should be the method.

It might be replied that drug use is *immoral*, while sex and fatty foods are not. It is morally wrong to ingest cocaine but not to have sex with your wife or eat a pretzel. Now it is quite unclear in what sense drug use is inherently immoral (as opposed to imprudent), but the relevant point here is that the law is not designed to punish immorality – that is, mere immorality is not sufficient to warrant enacting a law against the behavior in question. It is immoral to tell self-serving lies, to shout at your spouse, to belittle your friends, to betray confidences, to be rude on the subway – but none of these should be made illegal. Maybe drug-taking is immoral because it is the sign of a "weak character," but this is not enough to justify criminalizing it. Nor is the fact that drug use is potentially dangerous to the user a good enough reason to criminalize it, or else we would have to jail car drivers, skiers, and clumsy people. These actions are not the kind of thing that the criminal law has any business prohibiting. Imprudence and immorality are not in themselves criminally punishable matters.

The mistake in all these cases is to commit "the fallacy of deterrence." Some human activity has bad consequences – on that we all agree. We want to eliminate or reduce these consequences. So we threaten people with something very nasty if they engage in actions that lead to these consequences – namely, the criminal law. This, it is hoped, will deter them from the actions, and hence expunge the bad consequences. The trouble is that this is an extremely shaky argument: first, it is often doubtful that we will succeed in deterring people from doing these things; second, at what price is the deterrence enforced? In many cases we will have deterrence at the price of injustice. Perhaps the death penalty would deter a great many undesirable activities – but it would be ludicrously unjust to apply it to every such activity. Death by lethal injection for cigarette smoking? A law whose purpose is deterrence must always be backed by a demonstration that the law is *just*. The whole point of law is to guard justice – that is why it should command our respect. But the deterrence argument ignores the crucial role of justice in favor of a brute attempt to coerce by legal threat.

The primary question then is whether our laws against drug use are just – not whether they are an effective deterrent, or whether they prevent widespread suffering, or whether what they punish is a vice. There is plenty of room for doubt about whether our drug laws do achieve much benefit for the population – indeed, whether they produce more harm than good – but that is not the relevant question when considering whether drug use should be treated as a criminal offense with associated punishments. The question is whether the laws are just: whether drug use is the *kind* of thing for which punishment is appropriate, and whether the punishments meted out (often, substantial jail time) are proportionate to the gravity of the crime – which, broadly speaking, should concern the degree of harm done to others by the crime in question.

This criticism of our drug laws is not the same as the "libertarian" argument that people should be allowed to do whatever they like so long as no harm comes to others – that the state should be kept out of people's private lives. Whatever the merits of that point of view, it is not the same as the accusation of injustice: if a law is unjust, it is demonstrably wrong and unfit to be a law; if a law restricts people's freedom, that may also be a bad thing, but not necessarily because it is unjust to do so. Seatbelt laws may be an intrusion, a piece of unwanted state paternalism, but it would be wide of the mark to describe them as unjust – they are simply not punitive enough for that. Putting someone in jail for seatbelt laziness would be unjust, of course – but we don't do that.

Douglas Husak's book is devoted to the central question of the justice of our drug laws. He approaches this vital topic with a rare clarity and command, and a ruthless insistence on the exercise of rationality. In this book you will find not rhetoric and special-pleading, not politics and posturing, but a sober, open-minded, forceful critique of our current laws against drug use – indeed, of the whole idea that drug use is something that should be criminalized. As a philosopher, Husak sets out the foundational issues of justice and law with exemplary (and unsparing) lucidity, and presents a range of counter-arguments and replies that leave no stone unturned, however encrusted. He refuses to leave an issue dangling, offering us a thorough, highly informed, and sometimes passionate evaluation of contemporary drug policies. The combination of hard fact and rigorous moral reasoning provides a powerful indictment of what has been done in the name of law to police the use of drugs. Husak writes: "I think the sheer scale of incarceration of drug users makes prohibition the worst injustice perpetrated by our system of criminal law in the twentieth century. Only the institution of slavery and the despicable treatment of Native Americans are greater injustices in the history of the United States." (p.5) If you think this is an exaggeration, then read on: by the end of Husak's argument I believe you will find yourself convinced. You may then share his outrage; but, more importantly, you will have followed a resourceful, honest and reflective argument to its inevitable conclusion.

INTRODUCTION

This is a book, first and foremost, about the *injustice* of our punitive drug policy. It is not primarily a book about how that policy has *failed* – although I think that our drug policy almost certainly *has* failed. But saying that a policy does not work is a different kind of criticism than saying that a policy is unjust, and I am mostly interested in the latter kind of criticism. In any event, a number of excellent books about the failure of our drug policy have already been written. Many of these books contend that the United States is losing the "war on drugs," and insist that the war cannot be won. Even the best of these books, however, rarely discuss the injustice of our policy. Justice, after all, is not about winning or losing a war, but rather about whether a war should be fought in the first place. I argue here that relatively uncontroversial principles of justice give us good reason to stop punishing people simply for *using* illicit drugs. I conclude that our punitive drug policy is unjust, even if (somehow) it could be made to succeed.

The structure of the book is straightforward. In chapter 1, I describe our existing drug policy, and raise the questions that need to be addressed if we hope to decide whether it is just or unjust. I introduce *decriminalization* – the position I believe to be preferable on grounds of justice. In chapter 2, I list and critique several of the rationales that are frequently offered in favor of our present practice of punishing drug users. I argue that none of these rationales is persuasive. In chapter 3, I list several ways our policy of punishing drug users is counterproductive and detrimental to us all. I give reasons to doubt that we have a very good basis to predict exactly how our country would change if drug use were decriminalized. Fortunately, my argument does not depend on such predictions. We should endorse decriminalization because it is preferable on grounds of justice. From this perspective, I conclude that we should not continue to punish drug users.

LEGALIZE THIS!

Criminal laws against the use of drugs should be repealed – or, at the very least, not enforced.

More broadly, this is a book about how to evaluate the justice or injustice of our criminal laws. We cannot begin to appreciate why it is unjust to punish drug users unless we have a general understanding of when it is just to invoke the criminal law at all. I believe that we have come to rely far too much on the criminal law to attempt to solve our social problems. We overcriminalize and overpunish. Drug prohibitions are the best examples of these phenomena, but other examples could be given. We will not retard these trends unless we learn how to conduct a public debate about when justice allows or does not allow people to be punished. I try to make some progress in this direction. Like any philosopher, I continually assess *arguments* for criminalization. I conclude that we should be much less eager to enact criminal laws and to resort to punishment. By thinking about the justice of the criminal law generally, I believe we will be in a better position to appreciate the injustice of our drug policy in particular.

I try to avoid hyperbole in my defense of decriminalization. Prohibitionists have consistently exaggerated the dangers of illicit drugs and the advantages of our existing policy, and I have consciously decided not to match their inflamed rhetoric. But the sober tone of my analysis conceals the outrage I believe we should feel at the injustice of prohibition. Indeed, I think that the sheer scale of incarceration of drug users makes prohibition the worst injustice perpetrated by our system of criminal law in the twentieth century. Only the institution of slavery and the despicable treatment of Native Americans are greater injustices in the history of the United States. Ending prohibition will not be easy, and will require courage and leadership. The silence that accompanies this gross injustice – like the silence that surrounds most historical injustices – is nearly as shameful as prohibition itself.

1

UNDERSTANDING DRUG POLICY

CONFLICTING ANECDOTES

Discussions of drug policy – both those that support and those that challenge the status quo – invariably begin with anecdotes. There is an obvious explanation for why stories about particular individuals who use drugs are related so frequently. The experience of drug users varies enormously. The author can "prove" just about any conclusion by selecting the appropriate anecdote. In this book I argue that our drug policy is unjust. We should stop punishing people simply for using drugs. Like other authors who have written about drug policy, I begin with a few anecdotes. These stories help to put a human face on the drug war. They involve real people who have been treated unjustly by our punitive drug policies. Unlike most other authors, however, my discussion of drug policy does not place much reliance on these anecdotes. I do not pretend to *prove* anything by relating these stories. My central point is that we should be unwilling to draw any conclusions about our drug policy by generalizing from anecdotes.

Most of the anecdotes worth relating involve injustices to people who actually used drugs.[1] James Geddes admittedly smoked marijuana. In 1992, he was arrested while walking with a friend along a street in Oklahoma. The police got a warrant to search the home of his friend, where James had been a frequent visitor. The police found a small amount of marijuana, paraphernalia for smoking marijuana, and five plants growing in the vegetable garden. James refused to plea-bargain, maintaining his innocence. He was convicted and sentenced to seventy-five years for possession and an additional seventy-five years for cultivation, for a total of one hundred and fifty years in prison. On appeal, James persuaded the court that his sentence was excessive. It was reduced to ninety years.

Rob Pace, an eighteen-year-old college-bound honors student, was arrested in New Jersey for carrying drugs in his backpack during his class trip to an amusement park. After his release, the associate high-school principal refused to allow Rob to board the school bus for the ride home. School policy did not allow students caught with drugs to participate in school activities. Abandoned to contemplate the consequences of his arrest, Rob committed suicide by jumping between train cars. His note apologized to anyone who had been let down by his behavior.

Jimmy Montgomery used illicit drugs for medical purposes. A paraplegic who had been confined to a wheelchair for twenty years, Jimmy smoked marijuana to stimulate his appetite and control the spasms caused by the injuries to his spinal cord. In 1992, the State of Oklahoma sentenced Jimmy to ten years in prison for possession with intent to distribute the less than two ounces of marijuana found in the back of his wheelchair. The only evidence of an intention to distribute was the testimony of an officer who claimed that only dealers would possess that quantity of drugs. Eventually, Jimmy was released on a medical parole, and resumed his job as a mechanic.

Kory Ephriam of New York was shot in the back by a police officer in 2001. Police stopped the car in which he was a passenger and noticed a bag of marijuana on the floor. Kory had previously been arrested for marijuana possession. Rather than face arrest again, he fled from the car, with the police in pursuit by foot. Cornered behind a house, Kory was shot when he allegedly reached toward his waist. The car was not stolen, as police had suspected, and Kory was unarmed.

Records do not indicate whether Bruce Lavoie used drugs. In 1992, he was awakened by a battering ram that smashed through the room he shared with his young son in New Hampshire. A band of armed men rushed into his small apartment. Bruce was shot to death as he tried to defend his son. The police found one marijuana cigarette butt.

Other anecdotes involve sympathetic individuals who were punished excessively for their involvement in the sale of drugs. Miguel Arenas is a veteran of the Air Force who had never been in trouble with the law and worked as the manager of a railroad yard in Queens. In 1992, he was arrested and charged with taking part in a drug-selling operation among the yard's employees. Today, Miguel is serving fifteen years to life under New York's Rockefeller drug laws for selling two ounces of cocaine. The District Attorney in Queens who prosecuted Miguel remarked that "this was no choir boy" and "two ounces of cocaine is not a minor drug sale." But the state Supreme Court Justice who reviewed Miguel's sentence expressed dismay at what he was required to do under the mandatory provisions of the law.

Still other anecdotes involve people who were totally innocent of using or selling drugs. Accelyne Williams, a seventy-five-year-old retired minister, collapsed and died of a heart attack after having been chased around his home in Massachusetts by a police team conducting a no-knock raid. No drugs were found, and police soon learned that they had raided the wrong apartment.

Donald Scott did not smoke marijuana. Police shot and killed Donald after bursting into his California ranch, loaded weapons in hand. Aerial surveillance of the land had indicated that marijuana might be growing there, but no drugs were found in the home or on the grounds.

Of course, countless other anecdotes might be told to illustrate the horrors and excesses of our present drug policy. Many websites – such as that of FAMM (Families Against Mandatory Minimums) are replete with comparable stories. But my point can be made without the need to recount additional anecdotes. Justice should be the primary objective of a political system generally and of a system of criminal justice in particular. No person can possibly think that justice was done in the above cases. Despite these obvious injustices, many people believe that our drug policy is basically just and fair. How can anyone continue to support the status quo after such stories are related? The answer, of course, is that not all anecdotes about drug policy resemble the foregoing. Stories designed to support the opposite point of view can be related just as easily.

I might have begun my discussion of existing drug policy with the story of Sue Miller. Sue was a promising student when she began to smoke marijuana at age thirteen. She quickly graduated to harder drugs. Her grades plummeted. In order to support her massive cocaine habit, she stole money from her family and friends. Soon she dropped out of school altogether. Although Sue always believed that she could stop any time, her drug habit consumed more and more of her life. Her efforts to quit were successful for a while, but she always resumed her drug use at greater levels than before. Eventually, she robbed convenience stores and gas stations. She was arrested and released several times; her health deteriorated. At age twenty-nine, Sue died of an apparent drug overdose.

Both kinds of conflicting anecdotes are powerful. Our attitudes about drugs and drug policy are likely to be shaped by the stories we keep in mind. If we believe that the experience of James Geddes is typical, and the story of Sue Miller is unusual, we will probably favor a fundamental change in our drug policy. But if we believe that the experience of Sue Miller is typical, and the story of Rob Pace is unusual, we will probably favor whatever laws are needed to prohibit the use of the drugs we think are dangerous. My contention, however, is that we would be unwise to base our attitudes about drug policy on *either* kind of anecdote. For two reasons, we should resist the tendency that is so pervasive in the context of drug policy – the tendency to generalize from anecdotes.

First, stories similar to that of Sue Miller could be related about any number of activities that no sensible person proposes to criminalize. Some of these anecdotes do not involve drugs of any kind, while others involve the abuse of licit drugs.* We can all describe the terrible plight of skid-row alcoholics whose lives have been devastated by alcohol abuse. Some of these stories involve our friends and relatives. Despite these stories, no one wants to put people in jail or prison simply because they drink alcohol. Why not? One familiar answer is that "prohibition doesn't work." Frankly, it is unclear whether prohibition "works." In any event, this is not the *best* reason to oppose the prohibition of alcohol. Even if prohibition *did* work, we would *still* not want to put drinkers in jail or prison. The best reason to oppose the prohibition of alcohol is that punishing people for drinking would be unjust. We can believe that punishing people for drinking

---

*I use "licit" to refer to those drugs that are currently lawful for adults to use for recreational purposes, such as alcohol, tobacco, and caffeine. Illicit drugs are unlawful to use for recreational purposes.

would be unjust without denying the truth of tragic stories about alcohol abuse. We are aware that such stories describe exceptional rather than typical cases. We realize that the typical drinker does not become an alcoholic or wind up on skid row. We know that relatively few drinkers cause social problems that merit a punitive response. We do not generalize from anecdotes about alcoholics to formulate our social policy about alcohol.

Consider the horror stories that could be told about smokers of tobacco products. We all know people who have died of cancers and other diseases that almost certainly were caused by smoking. According to our best estimates, at least 430,000 Americans (and 4 million people throughout the world) die prematurely each year because of their use of tobacco – about ten times as many as die in traffic accidents and almost fifty times as many as die from using illicit drugs. Again, these victims include our friends and relatives. Programs to reduce the incidence of smoking are widely debated. Still, no one seriously proposes to put people in jail or prison simply because they smoke tobacco. Why not? Many reasons might be given. Perhaps tobacco prohibition could not be made to work. As before, however, the *best* reason is that punishing people for smoking would be unjust. We do not generalize from tragic anecdotes about smokers to formulate our social policy about tobacco.

Heart-wrenching stories could be told about activities that do not involve the use of drugs of any kind. We can relate anecdotes about people injured in ski mishaps, paralyzed by falls from horses, killed in airplane crashes, or seriously maimed in accidents on rides in amusement parks. We can tell stories about people who lived miserable lives and died early deaths because of their inability to control their eating. Every year, more than a hundred people die in their bathtubs. But we would be foolish to generalize from these stories to demand that criminal laws be enacted to punish anyone who engages in these activities. We all support measures to make risky behaviors safer. But criminal laws to prohibit these activities are never part of the equation.

The point is simple. We should not rely on anecdotes in making policy. Before we generalize from an anecdote to formulate a policy, we must be confident that the story is not unusual. The story of Sue Miller *is* unusual; it does *not* describe the typical experience of drug users. If we base our policy on her fate, we would be guilty of generalizing from a worst-case scenario. The tendency to generalize from such awful stories is all too common in contemporary discussions of drug policy. Throughout this book, I will try to compensate for this tendency by presenting more accurate generalizations about typical drug users. The evidence used to support these generalizations cannot be drawn from any single anecdote. I conclude that we cannot make much progress in thinking about drug policy by relating case histories of individual drug users. My critical examination of drug policy will not place much reliance on the anecdotes I have told. I hope not to lose sight of the fact that the policies we decide to implement will have a profound impact on the lives of real people. But I will not describe additional anecdotes in attempts to bolster my position.

Anecdotes are unpersuasive for a second reason – a reason that has nothing to do with whether or not they represent typical cases from which we should be willing to generalize. We must keep a crucial point in mind as we reflect on stories about how drugs – and our drug policies – have affected real people. It is important to realize that the criminal laws I propose to examine did *not* help Sue Miller. Her tragedy unfolded despite the fact that the drugs she used were illegal. Sue *was* punished for using drugs – on numerous occasions. Punishment did nothing to prevent her from becoming a victim of drug abuse. How, then, should her story persuade us to preserve the status quo – and to retain those very laws that failed to protect her? Why do such anecdotes dominate the writings of authors who support the drug war? The story of Jimmy Montgomery provides a pretty good reason to doubt that our drug policies are just. But how does the conflicting anecdote of Sue Miller provide any reason to erase this doubt? Anecdotes seem to be helpful in revealing the injustice of our drug policy, but how can they be used to show it to be just? Perhaps the real lesson to be learned from the story of Sue Miller is that our drug laws are unhelpful and ineffective.

Of course, those who support our existing drug policy purport to have an answer to these difficult questions. They admit that our drug policy did not prevent Sue Miller from succumbing to the evils of drugs. But they relate her story anyway, because they believe that criminal punishments for drug use are needed to keep *other* people from suffering a similar fate. Ideally, they would like to describe the experience of someone who actually benefited from our policy – someone who does not use drugs, but would have suffered from drug abuse if we had foolishly changed our existing laws. Of course, such people cannot be identified by name. They are like the drivers of cars who would have been killed at an intersection but were saved by the installation of a traffic light. According to this school of thought, criminal laws against drug users are needed to reduce the incidence of drug abuse, even though they do not help the millions of people who use drugs each year.

This is the explanation we must give if we want to understand why those who support our existing drug policy relate stories of how that policy has failed to help people like Sue Miller. This explanation introduces an entirely new rationale for our drug policy – a rationale that necessarily moves us beyond anecdotes. The focus no longer is on Sue at all. Despite the fact that her story is related in painful detail, the lesson to be learned is not really about *her*. Instead, the focus is placed on nameless individuals who might come to resemble Sue if our policy were altered. This explanation raises an important set of issues: How would a change in our drug laws affect the number of people whose lives would be like Sue's? Won't the repeal of criminal punishments for drug use increase the number of drug abusers? If so, how could anyone who has heard Sue's tragic tale favor the repeal of criminal laws against drug use? I will address these important issues in chapter 3. At this time, my only point is to caution against the tendency to support our drug policy because we are disturbed by anecdotes like that of Sue Miller. In order to approve of our drug laws, we must believe that they somehow protect *others* – even though they did not protect her. Clearly, the story of Sue provides absolutely no reason in favor of *this* belief. In fact, *no* anecdote can provide much evidence for this belief. These laws did *not* help anyone in the very cases that are related in the hope of persuading us to retain them.

For these two reasons, anecdotes do not take us very far. The fate of our drug policy should not depend on who is able to tell the most compelling stories. In order to give our policy the evaluation it deserves, we need to shift our attention away from anecdotes, and toward facts and principles. Public enthusiasm in favor of our drug laws often derives from misapprehensions about facts. If many of the things people believe about drugs were true, our policies would probably be justified. We would be silly to allow anyone to use a drug that does to a brain what a fry pan does to an egg, for example. But most of these claims are wild exaggerations and falsehoods. Just as importantly, public support for our drug laws often suffers from a lack of attention to the principles at stake. We call our institution of punitive laws a system of criminal *justice*. Why do we use that word? What makes *any* criminal law just or unjust? In particular, are our drug laws just? Anecdotes are not helpful if we insist that our thoughts about drug policy must be principled. Thus, I propose to move beyond anecdotes.

Justice was not served in the above cases. But anecdotes are not the best way to assess the justice or injustice of our drug policy. How, then, should we proceed?

ASKING THE RIGHT QUESTION

Like any philosopher, I believe that progress is made by assessing arguments. But we cannot begin simply by arguing. We need to decide what to argue *about*. We cannot hope to make progress on any topic unless we begin by asking the right question. In the present context, that question is: *Should drug use be criminalized?* Should we have a crime of drug use?* This same question can be expressed in various ways. A different version of this question is: *Should drug users be punished?* Should the criminal law punish people simply for using a drug? This is what I call the *basic question* that must be addressed in any attempt to evaluate the justice or injustice of our nation's drug policy. If we cannot provide a satisfactory answer to it, we should conclude that our current policy is unjustified and should be changed.

The main point of this book is to attempt to answer this basic question. This is the issue on which my subsequent arguments will be focused.

---

*Many (but not all) jurisdictions actually lack a crime of illicit drug *use*, and punish *possession* instead. I attach no deep significance to this fact. Laws are written in this way because possession is easier to detect and prove than use.

My basic question is about what the criminal justice system should do to drug *users*. It is *not* a question about what the criminal justice system should do to people who produce or sell drugs. Only if we first become clear about what should be done to drug users can we hope to provide a sensible perspective on those who distribute drugs. But I will not try to settle these latter issues here. I will not try to decide how, whether, or under what circumstances drugs may be produced and sold. I will be content to establish the conclusion that drug use should *not* be criminalized and that drug users should *not* be punished.

Before defending this conclusion, however, we must pause to try to understand the basic question itself. This question asks for a *rationale* for our policy of punishing drug users. Possible answers need not identify the motives that actually led legislators to enact laws criminalizing drug use. I will not examine historical documents that indicate why drug prohibitions were first adopted. The search for a rationale is not a psychological or historical quest. It is an attempt to find normative or evaluative reasons that can *justify* our policy of punishing drug users. I assume that all parties to the debate about drug policy are interested in deciding whether that policy can be justified.

In this section I will argue that people often fail to reach the conclusion I will defend because they begin by asking the *wrong* question. They start their examination of drug policy by addressing a different issue. This seems odd and surprising. The basic question I have asked seems straightforward and appropriate – even if it proves difficult to answer. Why would anyone purport to evaluate our drug policy by addressing some *other* question?

In the United States today, a national debate about our country's drug policy is underway. Growing numbers of knowledgeable and perceptive citizens have become dissatisfied with the status quo. Their voices can be heard on television and radio, and their opinions can be read in magazines and newspapers. They have written impressive books and joined various drug reform movements. Still, I fear that most public debates about our drug policy are less productive than they might be. Fair-minded and unbiased observers fail to reach the right conclusion because they begin by asking the wrong question. Too often, debates about existing drug policy address the topic: *Should drug use be decriminalized?* A different version of this same question is: *Should we stop punishing drug users?* I will try to show why this latter question is not the most basic question to ask in evaluating our drug policy.

The question I believe should be asked – should drug use be criminalized? – and the question that is generally asked – should drug use be decriminalized? – are different, and the difference is important. The right question demands a justification for existing policy. It asks whether we have a good reason for doing what we now do to drug users. The wrong question does not demand a justification for existing policy. It asks whether we have a good reason *not* to do what we now do to drug users. In a debate about existing policy, those who support the status quo gain an enormous advantage by beginning with the second question rather than the first. This advantage is wholly unwarranted. When debates focus on the issue of whether drug use should be decriminalized, critics of our policy are forced to identify the benefits of changing it. When they try to describe these benefits, their adversaries can raise doubts about whether these benefits will indeed materialize if our laws were altered. As I will show in more detail in chapter 3, it is very hard to predict exactly how our society would change if we stopped punishing drug users. No one should have much confidence in the accuracy of his predictions; too many unknown variables will affect the nature of a society in which drug use is no longer criminalized. The debate is likely to end in a cloud of uncertainty. Critics of our existing policy will not have been persuasive in demonstrating the advantages of change. In the minds of many fair-minded and impartial observers, defenders of the status quo will have triumphed. At the very least, the debate will end in a stalemate. No clear conclusions will have been reached.

Notice what is missing from the kind of debate I have described. First, this debate is almost certain to lose sight of principles of justice – the most important consideration to keep in mind when evaluating our criminal laws. A debate about the advantages or disadvantages of *change* is likely to become focused on whether existing policy *works* better than some alternative to it. Almost inevitably, the debate will center on how we can best attain the goals toward which we believe our policy should aim. Justice will probably seem unimportant if we are fixated on objectives.

Justice should not be conceptualized as a *goal* our policies should try to achieve, but as a *constraint* that limits what we are allowed to do in pursuing our objectives. In other words, justice rules out some strategies that we otherwise would be permitted to adopt in trying to attain our ends. When we concentrate on the different means we might employ to achieve our goals, justice can drop out of the picture. Small wonder that contemporary debates about our drug policy pay little attention to justice. As we will see, even the most outspoken critics of our drug policy tend to neglect the importance of justice. For justice to resume its central place, we must begin by asking the right question.

Something else is missing from a debate that begins by asking the wrong question. In a debate that asks whether drug use should be decriminalized, those who support our existing drug policy need not utter a single word in its defense. Their job is too easy. They can simply sit back and wait for their opponents to make predictions, and then challenge the accuracy of those predictions. Why do they win the debate when they have said absolutely nothing on behalf of the position they endorse? We should not punish people simply because we are unable to demonstrate the benefits of *not* punishing them. Any policy that resorts to punishment requires a justification. We should not assume that what we are doing is right unless someone can prove that it is wrong. We must always be prepared to show why what we are doing is right. If neither side provides good reasons, or if the reasons on both sides are equally persuasive, victory in the debate should not be awarded to the side that supports the status quo – when the status quo involves criminalization. Punishment is the most terrible thing that a state can do to its citizens; it is the most powerful weapon in the national arsenal. The criminal sanction should not be invoked casually; it always requires a compelling defense. Those who favor punishments for drug users must explain why they think this policy is fair and just. No one should be deprived of liberty unless there are excellent reasons for doing so. The basic question, then, is not whether we have good reasons *not* to punish drug users – so that drug use should be decriminalized – but whether we have good reasons to (continue to) punish people who use drugs.

My point is not simply that the burden of proof on this issue has been placed on the wrong side – although that is certainly true. Nor is my point that we should not allow one side in the debate to gain an unfair rhetorical advantage over the other – although that is certainly true as well. My point is that the debate cannot proceed sensibly unless it begins with a reason in favor of punishing people who use drugs. How can we possibly decide whether we should change our policy unless we know why we have that policy in the first place? Unless a reason to punish drug users has been put on the table, an opponent of the status quo has nothing to which he can respond. In other words, an effective argument for decriminalization must rebut the argument for criminalization. Without an argument for criminalization, there is nothing to rebut. Those who support a change in our policy are in the predicament described by David Hume, one of the most important philosophers in history. Hume wrote: "'Tis impossible to refute a system, which has never been explain'd. In such a manner of fighting in the dark, a man loses his blows in the air, and often places them where the enemy is not present."[2] Hume might have been describing the plight of those who challenge our drug policy.

Imagine the progress – or lack of progress – in a debate about any policy if its opponents were forced to describe the advantages of change, while its supporters were not made to defend the status quo. Imagine a debate about the institution of slavery prior to the Civil War. Suppose that abolitionists were required to make detailed predictions about how society would be improved if slaves were freed. Even the most eloquent critic of slavery could not have had much confidence in the accuracy of her forecasts. Controversy about these predictions would miss the most fundamental objection to slavery – its injustice. Surely, no one should conclude that the institution of slavery should be preserved because its defenders are able to raise doubts about the abolitionist alternative. At some point, defenders of slavery should be forced to defend slavery. Once a defense of slavery is on the table, abolitionists have something to which they can respond. They are in a position to show that the alleged defense fails to justify the institution. Unless some other defense of slavery is persuasive, the institution should be abolished.

What is true of slavery is true of any institution or social policy that (like our drug policy) resorts to punishment. At some point, defenders of drug prohibition must defend drug prohibition. If our criminal laws are to be *just*, each criminal law must be *justified*. To justify a particular criminal law is to provide compelling reasons to punish people who break that law. We need these excellent reasons – a justification for our criminal laws – because punishment is the worst thing our state can do to us. Punishment infringes rights and liberties that we usually take for granted. The justification must become more persuasive as punishments become increasingly severe – involving jail or prison, rather than a small monetary fine. We need very good reasons before we put people behind bars, and defenders of our drug policy must be pressed to tell us what these reasons are.

Sometimes we fail to demand a justification for our criminal laws because we mistakenly suppose that imprisonment is not really a major hardship. In the United States, we resort to severe punishments so routinely that we forget how devastating incarceration really is. We hear that criminals who are sentenced to a "mere" six months in prison are given a "slap on the wrist." Or we read that criminals are confined in "country-club" prisons. No one who has ever been jailed or imprisoned is likely to share these extraordinary attitudes. Prisoners lose their liberty and most of their rights. They are deprived of their families, friends, jobs, and communities. Their days are passed in unproductive idleness. Prison life is degrading, demoralizing, and dangerous. Once released, offenders are less employable, and often forfeit their rights to vote and to receive public benefits and services. Punishment has a negative impact on the lives of their spouses and children. These effects should not be imposed lightly. To ensure that our society is just, we must insist on a very convincing rationale before we resort to punishment.

Everyone with a serious interest in our drug policy should be urged to begin the debate by wrestling with the basic question I have posed. Ask yourself – and ask your friends and neighbors who welcome intellectual discussions – do you really believe that people should be punished for using drugs? Do you think that the laws that put people in jail simply for using drugs are justified? If so, why? Why does justice allow us to punish drug users? Don't suppose that you must describe the advantages of decriminalization until an argument for criminalization has been given first. If the question I have raised cannot be answered to your satisfaction, you should conclude that people who use drugs should *not* be punished – for no one belongs in jail unless a very good reason can be given to put him there.

Those who support decriminalization need not allege that drug use has benefits – benefits that cannot be achieved unless people are allowed to use drugs without fear of criminal penalties. Undoubtedly, drug use *does* have some benefits; I will return to this topic in chapter 3. But the case for decriminalization does not depend on whether drug use actually has these benefits, or on whether its advantages outweigh its disadvantages. The case for decriminalization is not that drugs are good. The case for decriminalization is that the arguments for criminalization are not sufficiently persuasive to justify the infliction of punishment. In other words, the best reason to *de*criminalize drug use is that the reasons to *criminalize* drug use are not good enough. This very simple explanation of why drug use should be decriminalized cannot be defended unless those who favor criminalization have made their case. Until they have told us what their reasons are, we cannot demonstrate that their reasons are not persuasive.

I admit that this case for decriminalization seems unexciting. It lacks the rhetorical appeal of calls to eliminate "taxation without representation" or to secure "one man, one vote." No lofty principle like freedom of speech or freedom of religion appears to be at stake. The "freedom to use drugs," or the "right to put any substance into our bodies" are unlikely to move citizens to action. But perhaps I needlessly denigrate my own argument for decriminalization. The principle I invoke – that no one should be punished unless there are compelling reasons for doing so – may be the most fundamental principle in a free society committed to justice for all. No principle seems more important in a state that takes punishment seriously.

This principle should be applied not only to our drug policy. *Each* criminal law must be justified. Where will we find these rationales? The burden to produce justifications for our criminal laws is placed squarely on *us* – the citizens of a democratic state. In our legal system, legislators are not required to give reasons for the criminal laws they enact. Citizens are forced to guess what legislators must have had in mind when they decided to resort to punishment by creating criminal laws. We should not be surprised that bad laws are more likely to be passed when those who draft them need not provide reasons in their behalf. We are relatively confident in the integrity of our judiciary because (appellate) judges are required to write opinions explaining how and why they decide cases. Judges do not simply affirm or reverse a judgment; they present their reasoning. Citizens can scrutinize their arguments; we can decide whether or not we are persuaded. Officials who are forced to publicly defend their reasoning tend to make better decisions than officials who need not explain anything to anyone. Criminal justice policy generally, and drug policy in particular, would almost certainly improve if legislators, like judges, were required to justify the decisions they make.

In the United States, we have become accustomed to a system in which our courts protect us from excesses by other legal officials. The rules of criminal procedure are especially important in ensuring that the police are not overzealous in enforcing the law. These rules derive from judicial interpretations of our Bill of Rights. Judges require the police to have good reasons to enter our homes, to eavesdrop on our telephone conversations, or to search our bodies. But the Constitution generally, and the Bill of Rights in particular, have not been construed to impose significant limitations on the criminal laws that legislatures may enact. Courts have shown extraordinary deference to legislative decisions to criminalize given kinds of activities. Judges do almost nothing to protect us from excesses by our legislature, and to ensure that the laws that police enforce are supported by good reasons.

In short, neither legislatures nor courts have developed an adequate theory of criminalization – a set of principles to govern whether conduct can be punished. Even more surprising is the failure of academics who study and teach criminal law to develop such a theory. Ask anyone who is knowledgeable about our criminal law to describe the criteria that must be satisfied before people can be punished. I am not referring to the procedures that must be followed before a bill can become law – such as the rule that it must be approved by a majority of legislators. I am referring to the *substance* or the *content* of the law – to the conditions that must be satisfied before the state can decide *what* to punish. The response to this question is likely to be a blank stare. Despite all of our political rhetoric about the importance of a system of law in which the power of government is limited, our legislatures are virtually unlimited in their authority to enact criminal laws that subject us to punishment.

This failure to develop a theory of the limits of the criminal sanction has contributed to the phenomenon of *overcriminalization*. We have far too many criminal laws in the United States – more than 300,000 at last count. The stigma associated with a criminal conviction has been diluted almost to vanishing point, since many new offenses punish behavior that is more laughable than reprehensible. For example, federal law imposes criminal penalties on persons who sell mixtures of two kinds of turpentine, walk dogs on the grounds of federal buildings, or disturb mud in a cave in a national park. It is much easier to pass than to repeal a criminal law, so the number of crimes grows steadily each year. Greater numbers of crimes help to produce more and more criminals, many of whom fill our jails. Over two million people are presently incarcerated in the United States. This statistic is a national embarrassment. Why are we so quick to resort to severe punishments? At what point will we decide that too many of our fellow Americans are behind bars? If we are serious about reducing the size of the prison population, curtailing the power of government and reversing the trend toward overcriminalization, there is no better place to begin than by scrutinizing the rationale for punishing drug users.

What *is* this rationale? We are not told, so we must guess. As I have indicated, this predicament is not peculiar to drug prohibitions. *No criminal law is accompanied by an official rationale.* Despite this fact, we should notice how easy it is to answer the basic question I have asked if we use almost any other crime – that is, almost any crime other than the crime of drug use – as an example. We send robbers, rapists, and murderers to jail. Suppose someone asks (rhetorically) whether people who commit these acts should (continue to) be punished. He challenges legislators to justify their decisions to enact these crimes – to provide a good reason to punish robbers, rapists, or murderers. His challenge is easily met. These people deserve to be punished because they have violated the rights of their victims and harmed them severely. We all have rights not to be robbed, raped, or murdered. Anyone who violates these rights *deserves* to be punished.

Because it is so easy to justify punishment when virtually any other crimes are used as examples, there is no real controversy about whether these offenses should be repealed. No sensible person opposes the punishment of murderers, rapists, or robbers. Good reasons for enacting these criminal offenses are easy to find. But the straightforward answer I have given in the cases of robbery, rape or murder is unavailable in the case of drug use. It is hard to see how James Geddes, for example, harmed or violated the rights of any victim by his use of drugs. What right(s) of which victim(s) did he possibly violate? Other drug users – Sue Miller, for example clearly harmed people and violated their rights. Of course, the harmful acts she performed that violated rights – stealing to get money to buy drugs, for example – are crimes already. We have good reason to punish Sue Miller, even if we do not punish her for using drugs. In any event, a rationale for criminalization must not only justify punishing *her*, it must also justify punishing each and every drug user. If there is a good reason to punish James Geddes – or any person who simply uses a drug – it cannot be the same reason we can give if we are challenged to explain why robbers, rapists, and murderers should be punished. Each and every one of these criminals has violated the rights of their victims.

What good reason, then, *can* be given to punish drug users? Eventually, I will conclude that no good answer has been provided. To reach this conclusion, we must critically examine the reasons that *have* been given. For that inquiry, however, we must await chapter 2. Before then, several more preliminaries must be addressed if we hope to decide whether our drug policy is just or unjust.

A FEW BAD ANSWERS

In chapter 2, I will critically examine a number of possible answers to our basic question of why drug use should be criminalized and drug users should be punished. Each of the possible answers I will discuss there is entitled to a serious reply. In this section, I will briefly describe two answers to this basic question that – despite their familiarity – are *not* entitled to a serious reply. Once we understand why some answers are bad, we are in a better position to appreciate what might count as a *good* answer. We cannot determine whether we have a good reason to punish drug users without some general thoughts about why anyone should *ever* be punished.

I have already described two bad answers to this basic question that are given frequently by defenders of the status quo. The first bad answer is really no answer at all. Without uttering a word on behalf of punishing drug users, prohibitionists raise doubts about the alternative of decriminalization, and pretend they have won the debate when these doubts are not resolved to their satisfaction. A real defense of drug prohibition must not take this short-cut; it must try to explain why our policy is justified. The second bad answer is "argument by anecdote." Those who support drug prohibition relate stories about people whose lives have been ruined by drug abuse. I have argued that we should not be quick to draw any conclusions from these anecdotes. The story may not represent a typical experience from which we should generalize. In addition, the story describes the devastation drugs have caused despite our efforts to prohibit them, and thus provides a dubious reason to preserve the very policies that have failed.

Many other bad answers to the basic question have been proposed. Lots of nonsense has been expressed on *both* sides of the drug debate, and we will do well to ignore it. Progress is possible only if we carefully evaluate the best rationales given by the most knowledgeable defenders of the status quo. In this section, I will describe some bad answers we are entitled to ignore – notwithstanding their popularity. First, many people seem to think that we are justified in sending drug users to jail simply because they have broken the law. Anyone who raises the question of why we should punish, say, users of ecstasy or cocaine, is certain to be reminded that the use of these drugs is illegal. This answer is also given when supporters of existing drug prohibitions are pressed to explain why we do not punish users of licit drugs like alcohol and tobacco. Drinkers and smokers are not punished because these drugs are legal to use. According to this school of thought, those who break the law must take responsibility for their actions and suffer the consequences. When no law is broken, there are no legal consequences to accept.

This rationale, of course, does not begin to address the question I raise here. We all know that drug users *are* punished; the disputed issue is whether they *should* be punished. In other words, we need to decide whether we are *justified* in punishing drug users. We do not provide a justification for what we do by pointing out that we do it. Nor do we improve on this answer and justify what we do by describing the process that enables us to do it. In a democracy in which our legislative bodies are elected, we presume that our laws represent "the will of the people." But even these laws require a rationale. When we refer to "the will of the people," we really are talking (at best) about the will of the majority. But what about the minority? How do we justify punishing members of the minority who violate the laws enacted by the majority? We evade this issue, instead of addressing it, when we say that our legislators need no more reason to punish people than that the majority wants them to be punished. We need to decide whether the laws that punish drug users should exist in the first place. Laws should be enforced once we are confident that they are justified. But first we must be sure that these laws should have been enacted. The fact that they *do* exist is immaterial; some rationale *for* their existence must be found.

Consider a debate about some controversial law in our own history, or in some other country. Several states in the United States once imposed criminal liability on persons who harbored runaway slaves. Some countries impose criminal liability on women who appear in public without a veil. Imagine debates about whether punishment is justified when these laws were (or are) broken. In the course of these debates, someone would be bound to point out that harboring runaway slaves or appearing without a veil is illegal. Obviously, this rejoinder would only baffle those who object to the law. They already know that punishment is imposed on persons who commit these acts. Their complaint is that the law is unjust and should be changed. Of course, this is the very complaint I make about laws that punish drug users.

Those who defend existing drug policy do not have a monopoly on poor reasoning and facile rationales. We should be equally wary of bad answers given by critics of the status quo. Many persons who believe as I do – that drug users should not be punished – reach this conclusion too easily. Some political thinkers – many of whom are *libertarians* – make their case against drug prohibitions by insisting that each of us has "the right to put any substance into our bodies." Our bodies belong to us, not to the state. They are our property. Therefore, these libertarians conclude, we have the right to do whatever we like to our bodies. Obviously, this right – if indeed we have it – is violated by laws that prohibit drug use. Therefore, drug prohibitions are unjust and should be repealed.

The issue is much more complicated than these libertarians suppose. We do not show that drug users should not be punished by claiming that each of us has a right to put anything we like into our bodies. To be sure, the fact that drugs are put into our bodies has some relevance to the issue of whether drug prohibitions are justified. We should be very reluctant to punish someone for what he does to his body. Ultimately, however, the justifiability of drug prohibitions depends on *what happens* when people put drugs into their bodies. Nearly all of the possible answers I will take seriously in chapter 2 cite the effects that drugs have on those who consume them, as well as on society at large. We can easily imagine a drug that we would want to prohibit, even though it is put into our bodies. If a drug kills us when we don't want to die, or turns us into homicidal monsters who victimize others, no one should think that we have a right to use that drug simply because these effects occur as a result of putting it into our bodies.

Ultimately, then, a good answer to our basic question depends on what happens to persons who take drugs. In other words, the justifiability of drug prohibitions depends on empirical facts about how users are affected by the drugs they take. What are the effects on drug users themselves? And how do drug users behave toward others? Empirical investigation is needed to answer these questions. Since the justifiability of our drug policies depends on empirical studies, it is easy to see why our basic question will prove so difficult to answer. The effects of drugs can be very hard to identify. Decades of research were needed to show that tobacco causes cancer, and the effects of illicit drugs can be even more difficult to detect. Any serious debate about the justice of punishing drug users quickly becomes immersed in disputes about matters of fact. In all likelihood, the empirical claims I will make will give rise to greater controversy than the principles of justice I will cite in my critique of prohibition.

Although empirical data about drugs are crucial to the case for or against criminalization, I will try not to overwhelm readers with facts and figures. Statistics soon become outdated, and excellent data are available elsewhere. The Internet contains dozens of sites with more updated information than anyone can possibly hope to assimilate. Although we still have much to learn, we now know more than ever about how drugs affect those who take them. What is the relevance of all these facts and figures to our basic question about prohibition? My central contribution is to address this question. I will provide a normative framework – consisting in principles of justice – in which this wealth of data can be assessed. Once we recognize the principles of justice at stake, I believe that the weaknesses in the arguments for criminalization will become apparent.

Notice that empirical facts and figures are *not* needed to justify other criminal laws. We do not require empirical research to decide that murder, theft, and rape should be punished. These harmful acts are justifiably prohibited by the criminal law because they violate the rights of their victims. We do not need to appeal to controversial studies to show that we have good reason to punish people who commit these acts. But laws that punish drug users cannot be justified in the same way. As I have said, drug users need not harm or violate the rights of anyone. Some other reason to punish drug users must be found, and any persuasive rationale will require accurate information about how drugs affect the people who use them.

We can avoid bad answers to our basic question by reflecting further about the justification for punishing robbers, rapists, and murderers. The justification for punishing those who commit these crimes is personal. In other words, the justification refers to facts about the criminal himself. Justice requires us to provide a rationale for punishing the specific individuals who are punished. If someone challenges us to provide a justification for punishing him, we cannot respond that our reason has nothing to do with him at all. We should not pretend that we have provided a personal justification for punishing James Geddes if we punish him for what Sue Miller has done. Nor do we provide a personal justification for punishing him if we describe the disadvantages to society that we fear would result if he were not punished. This rationale fails to respond to his challenge. This is not the kind of rationale we offer to murderers, robbers and rapists. They are punished because they deserve to be punished for the horrible things they have done. Does the drug user also deserve to be punished for the bad thing he has done? If not, his punishment has not been justified. In evaluating possible answers to the basic question of why drug users should be punished, we must keep in mind that any good answer – any persuasive justification for punishing him – must be personal.

The need for a personal justification of punishment is absolutely crucial to an assessment of criminal laws generally and to crimes against drug use in particular. If we do not insist that a justification for punishment must be personal, we will allow far too many unjust punishments. Two examples of unjust punishments should demonstrate why a justification for criminalization must be personal. First, consider *collective* punishments. A punishment is collective when each member of a group is punished for an offense committed by a single member of that group. Coaches of athletic teams favor these kinds of punishments. If any member of a team breaks a rule, each member of the team is punished. Next, consider *vicarious* punishments. A punishment is vicarious when one individual is punished for an offense committed by another individual. Terrorist organizations favor these kinds of punishments. If a parent or husband commits a transgression, their children or wives are punished. Why would anyone be tempted to impose a collective or vicarious punishment? The answer is obvious: These kinds of punishments *work*. Collective and vicarious punishments can be extraordinarily effective in reducing the number of subsequent offenses. If we really believed that punishment is justified whenever the failure to punish would increase the number of offenses, we would conclude that many collective and vicarious punishments were justified.

Of course, we do *not* believe this. We concede that collective and vicarious punishments can be effective, but we oppose them because we recognize them to be unjust. Justice constrains or limits what we are permitted to do in our pursuit of a goal or objective. These kinds of punishments are unjust because they do not provide a personal justification for punishment. Consider an individual who is punished (collectively or vicariously) when someone else has committed an offense. He demands a justification for his punishment. We would not answer him, and justify his punishment, by describing the disadvantages of not punishing him. These disadvantages represent an impersonal justification for his punishment; they do not show that *he* deserves to be punished for what he has done.

The need for a personal justification of punishment does not entail that *deterrence* is not a part of a justification of punishment. Of course, *part* of the reason we have a system of law in which we punish burglars, for example, is because we want fewer burglaries to occur in the future. But deterrence cannot be the *whole* justification for punishment. The goal of deterring drug use cannot be the complete answer to our basic question – for two reasons. First, we must know *why* we want to deter people from using drugs. I will discuss possible reasons why we may want to deter drug use in chapter 2. At this time, my only point is that we do not justify the punishment of drug users by claiming that we want to deter drug use. As it stands, this answer is no answer at all. It fails to get to the heart of the issue: Why should drug use be deterred? Notice again that this question is easy to answer if we use the crimes of rape, robbery, or murder as examples. These acts should be deterred because they harm victims and violate their rights. Protecting the right not to be harmed is perhaps the most central and important function of the state. But this is not the answer we can give to drug users who challenge their punishments.

There is a second reason why the objective of deterring drug use is a bad answer to our basic question. As we have seen, justice limits or constrains what we are permitted to do to people to in order to achieve deterrence. We are not justified in punishing someone simply because his punishment will deter others from doing something – even when we agree that we want to deter. If punishments were justified whenever they deter, collective and vicarious punishments would be allowed. These kinds of punishments work; collective and vicarious punishments deter. Before we are justified in punishing someone to deter others, however, we had better be confident that he deserves to be punished for what he has done. This is what I mean by saying that a justification of punishment must be personal. Punishment is unjust unless it can be justified personally – even though it may be extraordinarily effective in achieving valuable objectives like deterrence.

Prohibitionists frequently invoke impersonal justifications in attempts to explain why drug use should be criminalized. The need to deter drug use is cited by those who try to defend the punishments of the kinds of people described in my earlier anecdotes. Consider the remarkable rationale offered by William Bennett for punishing casual users of marijuana. Bennett proposed that the criminal law should be used not only against drug producers and sellers, but also against drug users – even the "casual" user who, he continues, "is likely to have a still-intact family, social and work life" and is likely "to 'enjoy' his drug for the pleasure it offers." If this person encounters no serious problems from his use of illicit drugs – like most drinkers of alcohol – why should the state punish him? Bennett's answer is that this problem-free, non-addicted casual drug user "remains an issue of national concern" because he is "much more willing and able to proseletize his drug use – by action or example – among his remaining non-user peers, friends, and acquaintances. A non-addict's drug use, in other words, is highly contagious."[3]

This rationale for punishing casual, typical drug users is among the most astounding statements to appear in the writings of drug prohibitionists. It is hard to take seriously a suggestion that the state should deliberately devastate the lives of problem-free citizens because other people might be led to imitate their behavior. In no other context would such a rationale be thought to provide a persuasive ground for punishment. Our prisons are full of people who are justifiably punished because of the horrible things they have done. There is no justification to add to this number by punishing people who have not done anything bad, but cannot be spared because others might be tempted to follow their example.

We will be more inclined to accept such impersonal justifications for our drug policy if we begin by asking the wrong question. When we inquire whether drug use should be decriminalized, we may be persuaded by an answer that describes the disadvantages that might result if we stop punishing drug users. But if we begin by asking the right question – should drug use be criminalized? – we are less likely to be satisfied by an impersonal answer. We must never lose our focus on the individual to be punished – as we lost our focus on Sue Miller in asking how her story could possibly persuade us to retain those very laws that failed to help her. Justice does not allow us to punish an individual unless he deserves to be punished for what he has done. Any good answer to our basic question – or a good answer to the question of why we should criminalize anything at all – must be personal, and show why someone deserves to be punished for what he has done.

THE CONCEPT OF A DRUG

I have referred frequently to "the status quo" and to "existing drug policy," but I have not yet attempted to describe that policy. We must understand the nature of our drug policy before we decide to retain or to change it. In this section, I will make a number of preliminary observations about contemporary drug policy in the United States. The task of describing our drug policy will turn out to be far more complicated than one might anticipate.

In the first place, we should be hesitant to say that we *have* a drug policy at all. In order to have a policy about *drugs*, we must be able to identify what drugs *are*, and to differentiate them from things that are not drugs. But no adequate definition of a drug exists. Let us examine the definition used in the statutes that regulate drugs. The definition in both the Food and Drug Act and the Controlled Substances Act basically contains three disjunctive clauses (that is, clauses separated by an "or" rather than by an "and"). It identifies drugs as "substances recognized in the official *United States Pharmacopeia*, or "substances intended for use in the diagnosis, cure, mitigation, treatment, or prevention of disease in man or other animals," or "substances (other than food) intended to affect the structure or any function of the body of man or other animals."

This definition is woefully deficient. Begin with the first clause – "substances recognized in the official *United States Pharmacopeia*." This definition identifies drugs by deferring to the expertise of persons with the authority to include or delete a substance from a book. It is like defining a word as any string of letters that appears in a dictionary. The problem with this kind of definition is evident. Strings of letters do not just appear in dictionaries; substances do not just appear in official registries. People have to decide whether or not to put them there. How do these people make their decisions? On what basis do they decide whether to include or delete a word from a dictionary, or a substance from an official registry? The definition is unhelpful in answering this question. In fact, political rather than pharmacological considerations have influenced their determinations. Tobacco appeared in earlier editions of the *Pharmacopeia*, but was subsequently removed in order to persuade legislators from tobacco-producing states to support passage of the Food and Drug Act in 1906.

The second clause – "substances intended for use in the diagnosis, cure, mitigation, treatment, or prevention of disease in man or other animals" – is even more obviously deficient. This definition is far too broad. It includes diagnostic tools like stethoscopes and preventive machines like treadmills. No one could possibly believe that a definition is adequate if it classifies such devices as drugs.

The third and final clause – substances (other than food) intended to affect the structure or any function of the body of man or other animals" – is better than the previous two. Before examining this definition more carefully, I want to comment on an oddity that it shares with the second clause. Both of these clauses – "substances intended for use ..." and "substances intended to affect ..." – make a curious reference to the intentions of some unspecified person. Can anyone really think that the status of a substance as a drug should depend on the mental states of those who produce or use it? According to these definitions, a placebo (or indeed any substance whatever) would qualify as a drug as long as persons had the appropriate intentions. Moreover, no substance – not even heroin or cocaine – would qualify as a drug if those who produced or used it lacked the relevant intentions.

The most popular definition of a drug used in medical circles deletes this curious reference to intentions and improves upon the third clause in the definition we have considered thus far. This definition is "any substance other than food which by its chemical nature affects the structure or function of the living organism." This definition contains four elements that are noteworthy. First, it rules out the possibility that a substance can be both a food and a drug. If a substance is a food, it cannot also be a drug. Second, this definition stipulates that the substance must affect the structure or function of people (I assume that people are the "living organisms" in which we are interested). A substance is not a drug if it has no effect at all, has only a "placebo" effect, or affects something other than the structure or function of those who use it. Third, this definition requires that the effect must be brought about by the chemical nature of the substance. A surgeon might alter the structure or function of a patient by using a saw to amputate his leg. But the saw does not qualify as a drug because physical rather than chemical processes bring about the alteration in the patient's structure or function.

For present purposes, the fourth element of this definition is the most significant. This element involves a feature the definition does *not* contain. This definition does not purport to use *the law* to distinguish substances that are drugs from substance that are not drugs. The definition makes no mention of the law at all. For this reason, this definition deviates from how ordinary speakers of English tend to identify drugs. Empirical studies indicate that respondents are far more likely to recognize a substance as a drug when its use is prohibited. Few Americans regard alcohol, tobacco, or caffeine as drugs, while nearly everyone recognizes heroin, cocaine, and marijuana as drugs. Politicians, in addition to the public, commonly use the law to decide whether a substance is a drug. William Bennett claims that "the majority of American city residents … do not take drugs." But he also cites statistics to show that alcohol is "the most widely abused substance in America."[4] These two statements suggest that Bennett is perfectly willing to categorize alcohol as a substance that is frequently abused – but not as a drug.

This alleged distinction between drugs and non-drugs has absolutely no basis in our definition. Nothing in the definition of a drug provides any reason to exempt alcohol, tobacco, and caffeine from the scope of a comprehensive set of drug regulations. Unquestionably, according to the definition I have cited, alcohol, tobacco, and caffeine are drugs. Recently, there may seem to have been a great deal of controversy about whether tobacco is a drug. But that is not really what the controversy has been about. Tobacco (or, more precisely, its active ingredients) is clearly a drug. Recent disputes about tobacco are political rather than pharmacological. The Supreme Court has decided that the Food and Drug Administration (FDA) lacks the authority to regulate tobacco, even though it has the authority to regulate drugs, because politicians did not regard tobacco as a drug at the time they created the FDA. This is a far cry from deciding that tobacco *isn't* a drug. There is absolutely no pharmacological basis for questioning the classification of tobacco as a drug. And what is true of tobacco is true of alcohol and caffeine.

The failure to distinguish licit from illicit drugs is unquestionably an advantage rather than a shortcoming of the foregoing definition. Surely the question of whether a given substance is or is not a drug should depend on its pharmacological properties and its effects on persons who use it, rather than on whether or how it is regulated by law. The status of a substance as a drug should not fluctuate as legal regulations are adopted and repealed. Opiates and cocaine were not suddenly transformed from non-drugs into drugs in the early part of the twentieth century, when the state first began to punish their use. Moreover, if we decide to allow people to use a substance that is a drug, it does not magically become something other than a drug at the moment its use is permitted. FDA approval does not transform drugs into non-drugs. More importantly, the whole point of this book is to question whether our drug policy is just. Surely this inquiry is sensible, even if my arguments turn out to be unpersuasive. If observations about our drug policy could not be applied to licit substances because they are not defined as drugs, the insights of reformers would be deprived of their full critical potential, and hard questions would be resolved by definitional fiat.

Despite this advantage, the foregoing medical definition is problematic. It is doubtful that a substance becomes a drug whenever it produces an effect on the structure or function of the living organism by its *chemical* nature. A lead bullet lodged in the brain may cause structural and functional changes through processes that seemingly are chemical. Should this bullet be classified as a drug? Moreover, the definition presupposes some baseline from which to judge whether structure or function has been *affected*. Is this baseline statistical, biological, normative, or some combination of the three? Is a lotion that blocks ultraviolet radiation a drug because it decreases the likelihood that the average user will contract skin cancer? Is a cream that prevents hair loss a drug because it reduces the probability that the typical user will become bald?

Most importantly this definition is too broad – and not just because it includes alcohol, tobacco, and caffeine. Many very familiar substances seem to qualify as drugs according to this definition, even though no one would think to classify them as drugs. Consider water or salt. Surely water and salt are substances. Surely they affect the structure or function of living people. Surely their effects are caused by chemical processes. If there is anything in the definition that shows these substances not to be drugs, it must be that salt and water are foods. Are salt and water foods? What exactly is a food? Is a food any substance that is ingested, and that people can't live without? People cannot live without some amount of zinc in their bodies. Is zinc a food? Surely not. Is zinc a drug? That, too, seems doubtful. But why not? What in the definition rules out this (presumably absurd) result? In light of these (and other) difficulties, this definition is inadequate. Unless some better candidate becomes available, it is fair to conclude that no satisfactory definition of a drug exists. When we purport to be talking about drugs, it is doubtful that we know what we are talking about.

One might anticipate that this definitional confusion would complicate endeavors to regulate drugs. How can we regulate what we cannot define? Surprisingly, however, current laws that govern illicit substances are largely unaffected by the lack of an adequate definition. The Controlled Substances Act – the source of most laws punishing drug users in the United States today – regulates "drugs or controlled substances." "Substance" is undefined, and a substance becomes "controlled" at the moment the Act begins to regulate it. Alcohol and tobacco are not governed by the Act, but not because they are not "drugs or controlled substances." They are not regulated because clauses in the Act specifically exempt alcohol and tobacco from regulation. *Anything* the Act regulates is a controlled substance. The question of whether a substance is or is not a drug turns out to be utterly irrelevant to the issue of whether it is subject to regulation under the terms of the Act. No definition of drugs is needed.

Despite the fact that our laws are not especially troubled by the lack of an acceptable definition of a drug, the definitional inadequacies I have described are not merely of academic interest. The difficulty of deciding whether given substances qualify as drugs has emerged as a major problem in public health. Any "health food store" contains a great number of substances that are alleged to be effective in treating various ailments and deficiencies. The manufacture and distribution of these substances often escapes regulation altogether – with grave health consequences to users. These substances often (but not always) are said to be "herbs" or "herbal remedies." Are herbs drugs? If not, is marijuana a drug? Return to the above definition. Like water and salt, the only possible basis for disqualifying herbs as drugs is that herbs are foods. Are herbs foods? Can they be both foods and drugs? Are they neither foods nor drugs?

Our best definitions of drugs are deficient. We do not really have a good idea of what a drug is. The plain fact is that, in many cases, we have no clear means to decide whether a given substance is or is not a drug. If we don't know exactly what a drug is, we may be unable to construct anything that deserves to be called a *drug policy*. As I have repeatedly emphasized, progress in a debate is possible only if we begin by asking the right question. Arguably, we will not make progress in answering the basic question I propose to address if we retain a concept – the concept of a drug – that we don't understand. Perhaps we should abandon this concept altogether.

The proposal to abandon the concept of a drug should be taken seriously. After all, what reasons do we have to want a policy that pertains only to drugs? Suppose we become persuaded that substantial risks to public health are posed by the use of a food or an herbal remedy. Why should the question of whether or how we should regulate these substances depend on whether we classify them as *drugs*? We should enact whatever regulations are sensible, however we ultimately decide to categorize the substances we decide to regulate. We can accomplish all of our regulatory objectives without using the concept of a drug at all.

The proposal to abandon the concept of a drug is radical – probably *too* radical. The concept of a drug is too entrenched in our discourse to be removed. Nor is it clear what concept we should substitute in its place.

Therefore, despite my misgivings, I will continue to suppose that our basic question is a question about *drugs*. I will pretend that the above definition is adequate, and that we are able to apply it to nearly any substance to decide whether or not that substance is a drug. I will assume that the question of whether a given substance is or is not a drug is important for public policy. I will continue to suppose that we *can* have a drug policy.

DRUG POLICY PRELIMINARIES

What, then, *is* our drug policy? The answer turns out to be extraordinarily complex; we can hope to understand our policy toward drugs only if we are prepared to draw a few distinctions. Unfortunately, most descriptions begin with the wrong distinction – a distinction that is not helpful in understanding our drug policy. We should not begin by distinguishing between those drugs that are "legal" or "illegal" to use. Only a handful of drugs fall neatly into one of these two categories. Most drugs are legal to use under some circumstances, but illegal to use under other circumstances. The most helpful distinction for understanding our drug policy is between the various *purposes* for which drugs are used. One and the same drug – cocaine, morphine, or prozac – is legal to use for some purposes, but illegal to use for others. The most fundamental contrast is between *medical* and *non-medical* purposes for using drugs. No one thinks twice about entering a drug store (now likely to be called a pharmacy) to purchase a drug (available by prescription or otherwise) for a medical purpose. But attitudes, reactions, and state policy can be entirely different when that same drug is used for some other purpose. The state often responds with severe punishments when drugs are used non-medically.

The distinction between medical and non-medical use invites further scrutiny, since it is so crucial in understanding our current drug policy. Drugs can be used for several different kinds of non-medical purposes. Some drugs are taken for religious purposes. Peyote is ingested in Native Americans ceremonies; alcohol is consumed in Christian sacraments. A comprehensive attempt to understand and evaluate our drug policy would require a separate discussion of each of the many non-medical purposes for which drugs are used. But one such non-medical purpose is especially important. I will describe this use as *recreational*. As we will see, it is hard to be precise in characterizing a given use as recreational. Roughly, people engage in recreational activities – whether or not these activities involve a drug – in order to seek pleasure, euphoria, satisfaction, or some other positive psychological state. When drugs are used in order to attain a positive psychological state, I will call that use recreational. The distinction between medical and recreational drug use is absolutely central to our policy. Drugs used for medical purposes are subjected to entirely different regulations than drugs used for recreational purposes.

The contrast between medical and recreational drug use is *not* a contrast between two kinds of drugs. Again, one and the same drug might be used either for a medical or for a recreational purpose. Therefore, the term "recreational drug" is potentially misleading. Since just about any drug might be used for a recreational purpose, a recreational drug can only be a drug that is *typically* or *generally* used for a recreational purpose. Alcohol is such a drug. Marijuana is another such drug. But since these drugs can be (and are) used non-recreationally, we should be reluctant to classify them as "recreational drugs." Instead, we should classify them as drugs with a predominant recreational *use*. To be precise, we should always use the adverbial form of the word recreational. The word modifies the verb "use," as in "to use recreationally," rather than the noun "drug," as in "recreational drug." I will not always be so precise; the term "recreational drug" is simpler than "drug used recreationally." But we must be careful not to be misled by this imprecision.

With the distinction between medical and recreational use in mind, the basic question I propose to address must be revised. Earlier I claimed that the basic question in assessing the justice of our drug policy is: Should drug users be punished? Now, we are in a position to appreciate that this question is somewhat oversimplified. Drug use, *per se*, is rarely a crime. No one would imagine that people should be punished for taking novacane in a dentist's office. For the most part, we are allowed to use drugs for a medical purpose. But when we use that same drug for a recreational purpose, we may be subject to severe punishment. So a more accurate formulation of the basic question that must be addressed in assessing our drug policy is: Should recreational users of drugs be punished? Should a person be punished when he uses a drug in order to increase his pleasure, euphoria, satisfaction, or the like? Should we enact criminal laws against those who use drugs to attain a positive psychological state? If so, why? These are more accurate versions of the basic question I propose to address.

But we still cannot begin to address that basic question. Yet another distinction must be drawn to understand the drug policy I propose to evaluate. As everyone knows, our drug policy differs enormously depending on *which* drugs are used recreationally. Prohibition is *selective*. The law responds very differently when caffeine, alcohol, or tobacco are used than when other drugs are used for a recreational purpose. No one seriously proposes that the use of these licit drugs should be criminalized. To be sure, policy about tobacco is changing rapidly. Joe Camel has been banished as an advertising symbol, and states are suing tobacco companies to recover the costs of treating diseases caused by smoking. But no one advocates that users of tobacco should be punished just for smoking. Eventually, I will return to the issue of how we might try to justify the differential treatment of licit and illicit drugs. For the moment, I simply note that our basic question must be refined still more. An even more accurate formulation of the basic question that must be addressed to assess our drug policy is: Should recreational users of *some* drugs be punished? If so, for which drugs should recreational users be punished, and for which drugs should recreational users not be punished? How should we "draw the line" between those drugs we will punish people for using, and those drugs we will allow people to use without fear of criminal penalties? A line must be drawn somewhere if users of any recreational drugs are to be punished; surely it is absurd to punish drinkers of caffeine, even if we are confident that caffeine is a drug and the purpose of the user is recreational.

In confining most of my focus to our policy about (some) drugs used for recreational purposes, I will have little to say about policies that apply to drugs used for other non-medical purposes. I will have nothing to say, for example, about drugs used for the purpose of committing suicide. One other non-medical purpose, however, is worth special attention. Many people use drugs in order to enhance their mental or physical performance. This use of drugs is neither recreational nor medical. Drugs used to improve the *mental* performance of healthy adults are still largely undeveloped, but certainly are on the horizon. When these drugs are perfected and made available to the public, society will have to wrestle to formulate a policy to govern their use. Imagine a drug that boosts memory but has a few bad side effects. Will students be punished for taking this drug during their college entrance examinations? Will employers be permitted to require their workers to take this drug in order to qualify for promotions? These problems may prove so hard that they will make our present questions about recreational drug use seem easy by comparison.

Of course, controversies about drugs used to enhance *physical* performance are already widespread. Anabolic steroids are the best examples. Since these drugs have a medical use, it is misleading to classify them as "illegal." Anabolic steroids are illegal only when used for a non-medical purpose – typically, to improve the physical performance of a healthy athlete. This use is rampant in our society. According to a recent survey, 40 percent of American boys twelve and over report that they have used, or plan to use, anabolic steroids in order to improve their strength and muscularity. Should the criminal law punish persons who use these drugs for this purpose?

I think not. Our decision about whether to allow or to prohibit the use of a given performance-enhancing drug depends on our rules of fair competition. Any mental or physical contest requires rules that specify the terms under which the competition will take place. Consider two examples. Students who take examinations may or may not be permitted to use books. Pole-vaulters may or may not be permitted to use fiberglass poles. There is no intrinsically correct answer to the question of whether books or fiberglass poles should or should not be allowed in these competitions. But the rules must take a position one way or the other on the issue, since it would be unfair to allow some participants but not others to have access to something that would be advantageous to all. In this respect, performance-enhancing drugs are similar to books or fiberglass poles. There is no intrinsically correct answer to the question of whether contestants in sports like football or bodybuilding should be allowed to use them. But the rules must take a position one way or the other. The criminal law should not play a role in enforcing these rules. Competitors who cheat by breaking rules should be failed or disqualified – but not sent to jail. Or so I believe. My main objective, however, is not to resolve the debate about the use of performance-enhancing drugs. I hope only to indicate that this question raises a very different set of issues than the question of recreational drug use I propose to assess here. Rules of fair competition play no role in deciding whether recreational drug use should be criminalized.

Since the response of the state toward drug users depends on the purpose for which drugs are used, one would hope that the line between medical and recreational purposes would be fairly clear. After all, a recreational user of a given drug may face severe punishment; nothing at all is done to that same person when his use of that drug is medical. So we need to inquire: *When are drugs used medically, and when are drugs used recreationally?* If the contrast between medical and recreational use proves very hard to draw, we can anticipate that the response of the state – which depends on this contrast – will prove difficult to justify.

When *are* drugs used medically? The most popular drugs can be used to illustrate the difficulty of answering this question. Consider caffeine – and try to decide when it is used medically, as opposed to when is it used recreationally. Why do people drink caffeine? Why do people typically prefer regular coffee, and why do they occasionally choose coffee that is decaffeinated? The obvious answer is that people tend to use caffeine when they want to attain a given psychological state – when they want to become more alert, more awake, or more energetic. Should we categorize this purpose as recreational? Perhaps – although I think that the question is hard. Consider a student who has never drunk coffee and who frequently becomes drowsy in his morning class. He complains to his friend, who recommends caffeine. He follows the recommendation, and finds that his problem is improved dramatically. Is it obvious that his use is recreational rather than medical? I am unsure. If the question still doesn't seem difficult, imagine that the friend is a doctor who "prescribes" caffeine. Is the caffeine now used medically rather than recreationally? Even the most typical uses of the most familiar drugs frequently elude categorization on one side of the line or the other.

Fortunately, we do not *need* to decide whether the use of caffeine is medical or recreational. Caffeine is among those drugs permitted either for medical or for recreational purposes. But the distinction between recreational and medical use becomes important when we consider other drugs as examples. We might change the story by substituting an amphetamine for caffeine. Suppose our drowsy student takes dexedrin rather than caffeine. This drug succeeds in helping him to remain alert in his morning class. Is his use recreational or medical? We have asked the same question as before, but here it is crucial, since state policy differs enormously depending on how we answer it. If his use is recreational, he is a criminal; if his use is medical, he is not. How do we decide which answer is correct?

As a society, we resolve this difficult issue through our system of licensing physicians and requiring patients to obtain prescriptions for many drugs. In theory, at least, the process is familiar. A person takes the initiative to visit a doctor, who conducts an examination and discovers the existence of a medical condition that warrants the use of a drug. As long as the user follows the prescription written by the doctor, his use of the drug is medical. In other words, the use of a drug becomes medical rather than recreational when a doctor authorizes it as such. As a result, our student who takes dexedrin is using the drug medically if he is able to persuade a doctor to write him a prescription because of his tendency to feel drowsy. Of course, the "familiar process" I have just described does not always conform to reality. Many prescription drugs are actually taken by persons who lack a prescription. The dexedrin taken by our student may have been obtained not from a doctor, but from a classmate who had a prescription. And many prescription drugs are used in ways that deviate from the terms of the prescription. Perhaps a majority of persons who use prescription drugs resort to what might be called *self-medication*. That is, they ignore the terms of the prescription, and use the drug in whatever way they believe "works" for them. If we define medical use of a prescription drug as use that is authorized by a doctor, all self-medication is non-medical. Under our existing drug policy, these persons are criminals.

One exception to the "familiar process" I have described is especially important. The trust we generally place in doctors to prescribe drugs for a medical purpose is withheld in the case of marijuana. Our policy does not allow doctors to prescribe marijuana, even if they are confident that their patients have a medical condition for which it would be effective. It is hard to see why politicians rather than doctors have the expertise to decide whether and under what conditions a given drug is likely to be helpful in treating a medical condition. Citizens and voters agree with this judgment. By a better than three-to-one margin, the public supports allowing doctors to prescribe marijuana for their patients. "Medical marijuana initiatives" have passed in each state in which they have been placed on the ballot: California, Oregon, Washington, Arizona, Alaska, Maine, Nevada, Colorado, Hawaii (by an act of the legislature) and the District of Columbia. Even in these states, the medical use of marijuana remains illegal under federal law, which prohibits the use of marijuana for any and all purposes. These initiatives provide ample indication of the extent of public dissatisfaction with our nation's drug policy.

At this point, however, I am not primarily concerned with unusual cases like medical marijuana, or with facts about what *really* happens to those drugs that are available only by prescription. I am more interested in the question of how doctors decide to write a prescription in the first place. Doctors make this decision after finding that the patient suffers from a medical condition for which the drug is likely to be effective. These medical conditions are called *diseases* or *illnesses*. Thus, the response of the state to the drug user – whether he will be punished or left alone – often depends on whether a doctor has found him to suffer from a disease or illness. The same drug used by the same person for the same purpose will raise no eyebrows at all, instead of resulting in a jail sentence, depending on whether the user has been found by a doctor to suffer from a disease or illness for which the drug is believed to be effective. With this answer in mind, return to my example of the drowsy student who drinks caffeine or takes dexedrin to remain attentive in class. I inquired whether his use is medical or recreational. We are now in a better position to understand how our society answers this difficult question. The drug use of the student is medical if it is taken to treat a disease or illness. If we cannot decide whether the student suffers from a disease or illness, we will be unable to decide whether his drug use is medical. *Does* the drowsiness of our student qualify as a disease or illness?

Obviously, this question cannot be answered without a theory, or a criterion, to distinguish those conditions that are diseases or illnesses from those that are not. We can evade this question by trusting doctors to draw this distinction. But we need to have some general understanding of how doctors do what we trust them to do. On what basis do they decide whether the drowsiness of the student is a disease or illness? In many cases, the determination that a condition is a disease is obvious and beyond controversy. No one challenges the classification of cancer as a disease. In a growing number of cases, however, we cannot provide a satisfactory answer to this question. If the contrast is nearly impossible to draw, the state policy that depends on this contrast will be nearly impossible to justify.

The line between conditions that are diseases or illnesses and those that are not – and the corresponding distinction between medical and recreational drug use – has always been tenuous, and is becoming harder to draw every day. The difficulty is compounded because drugs are no longer prescribed only for the treatment of a disease or illness. The conditions for which drugs are prescribed now include *syndromes* and *disorders*. Our confidence in our ability to recognize a medical condition when we see one evaporates in the face of the growing number of syndromes and disorders that are recognized today. What exactly *is* a syndrome or disorder? Many commentators have noted that we live in an era in which problems tend to be *medicalized*. That is, every problem is conceptualized as a medical condition, eligible to be treated with drugs. The phenomenon of medicalization is most pervasive in the United States, which leads the world in the consumption of licit drugs to change mood and behavior. Sexual conditions – and drugs used to treat these conditions – illustrate this phenomenon. Consider, for example, the controversy surrounding Uprima – a drug the FDA Advisory Committee voted to allow to be marketed by prescription. Tests indicate that this drug helps men to get erections, and to maintain them for a longer period of time than competitive drugs. Some thirty million Americans who would like to be able to engage in sexual intercourse report an inability to maintain an erection. Uprima is more effective than other drugs like Viagra because it operates directly on the brain. In other words, this drug, like those with a recreational purpose, is *psychoactive*. It works by increasing the levels of dopamine in a region of the brain that causes erections, rather than by facilitating the flow of blood through the penis.

The vote to allow Uprima to become available by prescription would suggest that this drug is designed to treat a disease, illness, syndrome or disorder. Does the inability to maintain an erection really qualify as a medical condition – the disease or syndrome of erectile dysfunction? How should we decide? After all, the condition this drug would treat has almost nothing to do with reproduction and everything to do with sexual pleasure. Uprima will be used almost exclusively by men who are beyond the age at which they want to reproduce. This drug is taken for purposes that seemingly qualify as recreational rather than medical. At the very least, this drug illustrates the extreme difficulty of drawing the line between medical and recreational drug use.

Consider yet a different product: Viramax. This substance is advertised to enhance sexual pleasure in both men and women. Advertisements assure us that Viramax is not a drug. This assurance is dubious, as I have suggested. This substance almost certainly satisfies each element of the most familiar definitions of a drug. Therefore, Viramax is (probably) a drug specifically marketed for the purpose of increasing sexual pleasure. Users need not suffer from some sexual dysfunction before they will be permitted to use it. The purpose for taking Viramax, by definition, is recreational rather than medical.

The inability to maintain an erection, or the difficulty of experiencing euphoria during sex, are hardly the only sexual conditions that are hard to categorize as diseases, illnesses, syndromes or disorders. Countless other examples could be given. Does the failure to attain an orgasm during sexual intercourse qualify as a medical condition? Would we classify as medical a drug that increased the joy of sex by producing orgasms? Or by producing multiple orgasms? What would we say about a drug that produced orgasms by direct stimulation of the brain, without requiring sex at all? How do we decide to answer these questions? What arguments should we make to try to persuade someone who disagreed with our answers?

Sex is not the only context in which the contrast between medical and recreational drug use becomes fuzzy. If a drug qualifies as medical when used to enhance sexual passion, what should we say about a drug that enhances the pleasure of other activities – such as eating, watching movies, or listening to music? Would a substance that relieved the boredom of housework like laundry and dishwashing have a medical use as well? How should we categorize drugs used for the many "eating disorders" that are now recognized? If someone eats too fast, experiences guilt over eating too much, eats when not hungry, or is heavier than he would like, he may suffer from "binge eating disorder" – a condition for which antidepressants may be prescribed. Are these drugs used medically? These questions are important, because people who use these same drugs for recreational purposes can be sent to prison. Some of the questions I have asked are fanciful at the present time. But there is no reason to believe that pharmaceutical companies are incapable of creating substances that add to the pleasure of everyday tasks or help us to attain the kind of body shape we desire. If existing drugs do not demonstrate the difficulties of drawing the line between recreational and medical use, we can be sure that new drugs are on the horizon that will blur that line to the vanishing point.

Of course, many of the questions I have raised are *not* fanciful. Clearly, the difficulties I have identified jeopardize the supposition that illicit drugs are used primarily for recreational purposes. Many people use ecstasy for the very same reason they use Viramax – to enhance their sexual pleasure. They use cocaine for the same reason they use caffeine – to remain alert. They use marijuana for the same reason they use amphetamines – to overcome the tedium of routine, everyday tasks. At the present time, doctors are not permitted to prescribe most of these drugs because they are said to have no medical use. I have tried to raise doubts about how to understand the elusive concept of "medical use." Without a better theory of disease or illness, it is impossible to decide when a drug is used medically as opposed to recreationally.

When a distinction proves virtually impossible to draw, we should review our reasons for trying to draw it. Why should it really *matter* whether a drug is used for a medical or a recreational purpose? As I have indicated, our present drug policy attaches extraordinary significance to this distinction. Persons who use barbiturates medically are left alone; persons who use them recreationally can be punished. Eventually, of course, I want to assess and evaluate our drug policy, not merely describe it.

Why should our policy place such enormous weight on the distinction between medical and recreational use? What is there about recreational drug use, as opposed to medical drug use, that could possibly justify a punitive state response?

Ultimately, I do not believe that a satisfactory answer can be given. The distinction between recreational and medical use, which has proved so hard to draw, is probably not worth preserving as a cornerstone of our drug policy. In other words, this distinction cannot bear the great weight that our existing policy has placed upon it. Obviously, those who support our present drug policy do not agree. They continue to apply totally different regulations to drugs used for a medical purpose than to drugs used for a recreational purpose – even when the very same drug is involved. Why does anyone struggle to try to draw the elusive line between medical and recreational drug use? In chapter 3, I will say more about the motivation for trying to draw this distinction. At this point, I simply mention the extraordinary significance our drug policy attaches to the contrast between medical and recreational drug use. We cannot hope to understand our drug policy without thinking carefully about this distinction.

I fear that my efforts to describe our existing drug policy have confused the topic more than they have clarified it. I began by questioning whether we have a drug policy at all, largely because we have no precise definition of what a drug is. Then, I introduced the fundamental distinction between recreational and medical drug use. Although this distinction is absolutely crucial to our present policy, it is far from clear when a drug is used recreationally, and when a drug is used medically. We tend to rely on doctors to draw this troublesome contrast. A drug is used medically when it is taken in the treatment of a disease or illness. Unfortunately, we lack a good theory of when a condition is a disease or illness. In light of these problems, I questioned whether the distinctions on which our policy depends are worth trying to salvage. This question, however, begins to cross the threshold from a description to an evaluation of our drug policy. We can anticipate, however, that a policy that is based on the distinctions I have drawn will prove enormously hard to justify.

PUNISHMENT AS POLICY

I have tried to refine the basic question that must be answered if we hope to evaluate the justice of our drug policy: Should the recreational use of (some) drugs be criminalized? Should a person be punished when he uses (some) drugs in order to increase his pleasure, euphoria, satisfaction, or the like? If so, why?

The previous section provides ample indication that several aspects of our drug policy are mysterious and difficult to comprehend. But one thing about our policy is crystal clear. When we are convinced that a given drug (other than alcohol, caffeine, or tobacco) is used for a recreational purpose, the response of our state is extraordinarily punitive. Both friends and foes of this policy frequently describe it as a *war* on drugs – or, more precisely, as a war on people who use drugs for recreational purposes. I believe that this description of our policy is overblown and inflammatory; I will not make much use of the "war" metaphor in what follows. That aspect of our drug policy I purport to evaluate is better described simply as *selective drug prohibition*.

The toll of our prohibitory policy is often conveyed by anecdotes. People like Donald Scott are sometimes described as casualties or innocent victims of the drug war. In this section, I will briefly describe this toll with a few facts and figures. Eyes may glaze when these statistics are presented. Still, the following account is necessary if we hope to understand our policy. Even those who are familiar with these facts and figures can be shocked each time the data are updated.

We are in the midst of the most punitive period in American history. The total population in our jails and prisons has recently surpassed two million – more than triple the number of 1980. No democracy has ever attempted to govern itself with such a large percentage of its population behind bars. We pay a staggering price for our eagerness to resort to incarceration. In 2000, the United States spent about forty billion dollars on prisons and jails. In our largest states, the prison budget easily exceeds the expenditures for higher education. Much of the growth in imprisonment is due to increasingly severe punishments for non-violent criminals, and for drug offenders in particular. Under federal law as well as in several states, drug crimes now receive harsher punishments than many violent assaults, rapes, or homicides. By 2000, approximately 460,000 drug offenders were incarcerated – about the same number as the *entire* prison population in 1980. Nearly one of every four prisoners in America is behind bars for a non-violent drug offense. This ratio has climbed dramatically. In 1986, about eighteen of every 100,000 American citizens was imprisoned for a drug offense. A decade later, that figure had jumped to sixty-three. From 1980 to 1997, the number of non-violent offenders in state prisons tripled, while the number of drug offenders increased elevenfold. In each year since 1988, more drug offenders than violent criminals have been sent to prison. Federal law enforcement agencies in particular have become obsessed with drugs. Federal agencies with responsibilities for law enforcement made over 30,000 arrests for drug offenses in 1999; only about 5,000 arrests were made for violent crimes. About 58 percent of all federal inmates are incarcerated for drug offenses, and prison terms have increased from an average of sixty-two months to seventy-four months from 1984 to 1999. These data prompted General Barry McCaffrey, the drug czar of the United States, to characterize the prison system in the United States as an American gulag.

Although results vary from one jurisdiction to another, most drug offenders sentenced to prison sell drugs. But 28 percent of all offenders sentenced to state prisons were convicted of simple possession and use. There is no trend in law enforcement to shift resources away from casual users toward the arrest and prosecution of higher-level drug offenders. In our era of "zero-tolerance," the crime of simple possession remains the meat and potatoes of our drug policy. Sentences are harsh. Under federal law, the severity of punishment is derived from the complex interaction of sentencing guidelines with mandatory minimum statutes. Prior to 1986, federal judges retained broad flexibility to tailor sentences for drug offenders to the particular circumstances of the offender. The Anti-Drug Abuse Act of 1986 dramatically transformed the sentencing of drug offenders by imposing mandatory minimum sentences, eliminating the possibility of probation or parole for most offenses, and increasing terms of incarceration. This Act mandated a five- to forty-year sentence, with no possibility of parole, for first offenders convicted of possession with intent to distribute relatively small quantities of designated drugs (for example, ten grams of PCP or one gram of LSD, even if these drugs are diluted in mixtures). Sentences of ten years to life, with no possibility of parole, were mandated for first offenders convicted of possession with intent to distribute large quantities of drugs. Amendments to the Act in 1988 imposed mandatory minimums for simple possession offenses, provided for the eviction of public housing residents if any member or guest of the household was involved in given drug offenses, and established the death penalty for persons engaged in "continuing criminal enterprises" who commit or solicit the commission of murder. The Violent Crime Control and Law Enforcement Act of 1994 significantly increased mandatory minimums for possession offenses still further, and authorized capital punishment for several new offenses. Mandatory minimums were doubled for defendants with a prior conviction for a drug felony, and were increased yet again if drugs were distributed to a person under twenty-one, to a pregnant woman, or near a school or video-arcade facility.

Rates of incarceration tell only part of the story about our punitive drug policies. In addition to imprisonment, drug users are often required to pay restitution, undergo treatment, lose their financial aid in school, or perform community service. More than half of the states have enacted laws that allow the licenses of drivers to be suspended for the offense of drug possession. Mere investigation for a possession offense can result in the forfeiture of property, including a home. In some states, drug users can be denied welfare benefits or be evicted from public housing, including homeless shelters.

Punishments often involve marijuana, the least harmful but most commonly used illicit drug. In federal courts, over two-thirds of all sentences for simple drug possession involved marijuana. Among the fifty states, the response to marijuana use varies enormously. In ten states, possession of small amounts of marijuana is punishable only by a fine. In several other states, incarceration is an option that is rarely exercised. Nonetheless, the trend is toward incarceration for the crime of marijuana use and posses- sion.[5] Between 1991 and 1995, arrests for the use of marijuana doubled in the United States. By 1999, over 700,000 persons were arrested for marijuana offenses. New York City led the nation in these arrests, 88 percent of which were for simple possession.

Admittedly, most persons arrested for using marijuana in places like New York City are *not* actually punished according to the definition of punishment I presuppose here. But even those users who are not prosecuted run afoul of the criminal justice system. They are typically arrested, detained overnight, searched, and generally inconvenienced. Their drugs are confiscated. This mistreatment would be illegal unless users could be charged with a criminal offense. The fact that few jurisdictions have the resources to prosecute the massive numbers of drug users who are caught does not negate the major disruption that the enforcement of prohibition causes to their lives.

Punitive polices continue to be implemented when new drugs gain unfavorable publicity. Federal convictions for offenses involving ecstasy have grown 745 percent from 1998 to 2000, and are expected to skyrocket still more in subsequent years. New penalties mandated under the Ecstasy Anti-Proliferation Act of 2000 treat the drug more harshly than powder cocaine offenses. On a per-dose basis, ecstasy crimes are punished more severely than those involving heroin.

International comparisons help to put the above figures in perspective. The rate of incarceration in the United States is perhaps the highest in the world (although the rate in Russia may be higher). Nearly one of every four people behind bars resides in the United States – even though it has only 5 percent of the world's population. Punishments for drug offenses are the most severe in the Western industrialized world. America's imprisonment of drug offenders (460,000) is far greater than total prison population in the whole European Union (357,000) – even though Europe has about 100 million more people than the United States. To a large extent, this differential is explained by a more sensible policy toward users of marijuana. No criminal penalties for marijuana possession and use are imposed in Italy, Spain, Switzerland, Ireland, and parts of Germany and Austria. In Portugal, no one can be imprisoned for the use or possession of any illicit drug.

Despite the severity of punishments in the United States, we should be reminded that the vast majority of illicit drug users are undetected.

Approximately 15 million Americans use an illicit drug each month. Every day, about 6,400 Americans try marijuana for the first time. Few are ever arrested. This is true even of users of "harder" drugs. About seven-eighths of frequent cocaine and heroin users are never apprehended. Obviously, our jails could not begin to accommodate all illicit drug users.

Any thoughtful American should be appalled by these facts and figures. Many have come to believe that the policy of drug prohibition represents a colossal waste of money. They are almost certainly correct. The cost of incarcerating nonviolent drug offenders is enormous. But the price tag of drug prohibition is not measured simply by the expense of maintaining our jails and prisons. Public assistance is expended on the families of inmates who have lost their breadwinner. Tax dollars are spent on ineffective prevention programs like DARE (Drug Abuse Resistance Education). Personal incomes are untaxed because drug markets must operate underground. Attorneys are paid to prosecute or defend people correctly or incorrectly accused of drug offenses. Still, the *real* cost of drug prohibition is not the money spent by citizens and taxpayers, but the impact on the lives of drug users. The true casualties of the drug war are the many people whose anecdotes I briefly related at the beginning of this chapter. I will argue that our punitive drug policies are unjust, and that we have no good reason to punish the hundreds of thousands of persons we have imprisoned for the crime of using illicit drugs.

THE RIGHT ANSWER: DECRIMINALIZATION OF DRUG USE

I will defend a negative answer to our basic question: "Should the recreational use of (some) drugs be criminalized?" Drug users should *not* be punished. Proving a negative is notoriously difficult; showing that there is no good reason to punish drug users is probably impossible. All that can be done is to identify the deficiencies in the several answers that prohibitionists have actually given. In chapter 2, I will examine four such answers. I will argue that none of them can justify our existing drug policy. In other words, none of them provides a good reason to punish those who use drugs for recreational purposes. Before evaluating these answers, however,

I want to describe the conclusion I favor – the position to which we are committed if I am correct that no good rationale for drug prohibition can be found.

This position is *decriminalization*. Unfortunately, this term (like *legalization*, which sometimes is taken to be equivalent to it) has no standard definition. Even lawyers are confused about what is meant when they are told that a jurisdiction or country has "decriminalized drugs." Disagreement and uncertainty about its meaning has clouded the debate about whether decriminalization should be implemented. Such confusion helps to explain the wildly different results that are reported when the public is polled about drug policy. Many polls have asked whether the use of, say, marijuana should be decriminalized. According to a Gallup Poll in August of 2001, 34 percent of all Americans answered that the use of marijuana should be legalized – the highest level of support in at least thirty years. When the question is altered to whether people should be punished just for using marijuana, fewer respondents support the status quo. Although the public does not approve of "making marijuana legal," it is less enthusiastic about punishing drug users. These two questions, as I understand them, are one and the same. These results illustrate a familiar phenomenon – respondents answer the same question differently, depending on how it is phrased. When the question is altered still further, so that American adults are asked whether users of marijuana should be eligible for jail or prison, some polls indicate that a majority of respondents oppose our drug policy. Later, I will return to the significance of public opinion surveys. At this time, my only point is that the combination of answers I have described is evidence of profound confusion about the meaning of terms like legalization and decriminalization.

Since this word means different things to different people, it is essential to explain what I take decriminalization to be. As I propose to define it here, the idea of decriminalization is clear and simple. Drug decriminalization means that the use of a drug for recreational purposes would no longer be a crime. No one would be punished just for using a drug recreationally. The behavior of James Geddes would not subject him to arrest and prosecution. Although the core idea of decriminalization is remarkably straightforward, a great deal of confusion results from mistaken assumptions about what decriminalization entails. In this section, I will discuss what decriminalization does *not* mean. I will describe eight issues that are not resolved by a commitment to decriminalization. Numerous policy alternatives turn out to be compatible with decriminalization as I define it here. We can better appreciate what decriminalization means when we avoid the various ways it is distorted and misconstrued.

I

Confusion about decriminalization results partly from a lack of agreement about what it means for something to be a crime. Surprisingly, even scholars and practitioners of criminal law are uncertain about what might be called the *nature of the criminal law*. That is, they are unclear about what makes conduct criminal, about the criteria that must be satisfied before conduct qualifies as a crime. My own approach to this issue – to the problem of specifying the nature of the criminal law – draws heavily on the concept of punishment. When conduct is criminalized, persons who engage in it become subject to punishment. If these persons are not subject to punishment, then their conduct has not been prohibited by the criminal law. Therefore, if we know what punishment is, we will know whether something is a crime.

This approach, however, does not solve the problem, since confusion about the nature of the criminal law resurfaces at a new level. If we are uncertain about whether a given way of being treated is a kind of punishment, we will be uncertain about whether the behavior that allows people to be treated in this way has been criminalized. In most cases, we are not at all unclear about this. If someone commits armed robbery and is sentenced to prison, we have no doubt that he has been punished for a crime. Often, however, we are uncertain about whether what we do to people amounts to a punishment. When we are unclear about this, we should also be unclear about whether what that person has done is a crime. Traffic offenses are good examples of this uncertainty. Someone who exceeds the time limit on a parking meter is given a ticket and is made to pay a monetary fine. Is this fine a punishment? If not, overtime parking is not a crime; if so, overtime parking is a crime. There is no simple answer to this question. Tickets and small monetary fines have some but not all of the characteristics of punishments. Traffic offenses such as overtime parking have some but not all of the characteristics of crimes. We might call these offenses *quasi-crimes*.

I mention the problem of specifying the nature of the criminal law because it complicates our understanding of drug decriminalization. Drug decriminalization, as I define it here, means that recreational drug use is no longer a crime. If recreational drug use is no longer a crime, people will not be punished for using drugs recreationally. Beyond this simple point, the issue becomes murky. What kinds of state responses to recreational drug users are modes of punishment, and therefore ruled out by decriminalization? I hope not to lose sight of what is clear about the idea of decriminalization by becoming immersed in this difficult question. Drug decriminalization means that no form of punishment – whatever exactly punishment is taken to be – should be imposed on people simply because they use a drug for recreational purposes. If we think that a ticket paid by a monetary fine is *not* a mode of punishment, then we can accept that recreational drug users might be given tickets even though drug use has been decriminalized. But if we think that a ticket paid by a monetary fine *is* a mode of punishment, then we cannot endorse decriminalization while allowing recreational drug users to be given tickets.

This debate about the nature of the criminal law is not solely of academic interest. Consider, for example, the confusion that has surrounded the announcement in England in October of 2001 that cannabis (marijuana) would be reclassified from a class B to a class C drug. Under this new proposal, which is likely to become effective in 2002, those who possess cannabis will no longer be arrested. Still, persons suspected of possession can be searched, and their cannabis can be seized. They can be summoned to appear in court, and are subject to a maximum term of imprisonment for two years. This proposed change is of major significance. England has the toughest drug laws in Europe; nearly 100,000 people are arrested for the crime of possession each year. About 70 percent of these arrests were for cannabis possession. But does this new policy amount to the decriminalization of marijuana? Does it at least take a step toward decriminalization? David Blunkett, the politician who proposed the reclassification, insists that it does not. Still, many others – both those who favor and those who oppose the change – describe the proposal as "decriminalization by a different name." The confusion, of course, is in understanding what is meant by decriminalization.

The debate about the nature of the criminal law is also crucial when reformers propose that recreational drug users should be given *treatment*. I do not have in mind the proposal that treatment should be made available to any recreational drug user who wants it. This proposal is sensible. According to the Office of the National Drug Control Policy (ONDCP), only about 40 percent of all addicts who need treatment actually receive it. The issue that arises here, however, involves a very different proposal – to *require* treatment as an *alternative* to punishment. The movement to "treat, not punish," continues to gain momentum. Consider, for example, Proposition 36, approved by a three to two margin by California voters in 2000. This Proposition requires anyone caught using illicit drugs to subject himself to treatment. Failure to undergo treatment, or to undergo treatment successfully, subjects the drug user to criminal liability and punishment. The movement to "treat, not punish" is not confined to California. Throughout the United States today, somewhere between 1 and 1.5 million Americans are coerced into twelve-step alcohol and drug treatment programs, often because they "choose" to participate rather than face jail or prison.[6] Treatment is an option many states offer as a way to avoid incarceration. Such proposals are generally regarded as humane alternatives to punishment. Sponsors of Proposition 36 argued that 36,000 fewer people would be imprisoned each year simply for possessing illicit drugs.

I will return to the topic of drug treatment in chapter 3. At this time, the difficulty with such proposals should be apparent: Mandatory treatment is not an alternative to punishment; it is a different mode of punishment. Support for decriminalization is incompatible with treatment as a forced alternative to punishment. No one who favors decriminalization can approve of mandatory drug treatment, unless he believes that coerced treatment is not a mode of punishment. Decriminalization does not allow the state to sentence drug users to treatment any more than it allows drug users to be sentenced to jail. I have little doubt that treatment is preferable to incarceration if we must choose between the two. But we need not make this choice. We need not assume that recreational drug users must either be bad – and deserve punishment – or sick – and need treatment. If I am correct, what should our criminal justice system do to people who use drugs recreationally? The answer given by those who endorse decriminalization is straightforward and simple: Nothing. Decriminalization places the phenomenon of recreational drug use *per se* beyond the reach of the criminal law.

Because I categorize both mandatory treatment as well as a ticket paid by a monetary fine as kinds of punishments, I regard them as incompatible with decriminalization. But we need not insist on that categorization here. In a world in which drug use has been decriminalized, our policy toward recreational drug users might come to resemble our policy toward parking offenders. Recreational drug use might become a quasi-crime. Alternatively, (strange as it may seem) our policy toward recreational drug users might come to resemble our policy toward persons found not guilty of a crime by reason of mental illness. On this model, recreational drug use provides a justification for coerced treatment. To be sure, anyone who believes that our current policies are unjust would regard the alternative of ticketing or treating recreational drug users as an improvement over the status quo. By almost any measure, small fines or mandatory treatments are less unjust than the severe sentences currently imposed on recreational drug users. But these alternatives, however preferable to existing policy, are not the positions I favor. From my perspective, fines and coerced treatment are kinds of punishments – albeit less severe.

Again, however, such matters as whether recreational drug users may be given tickets or required to undergo treatment are relatively minor details that should not obscure what is crystal clear about decriminalization. What is beyond controversy is that a sentence of jail or prison for recreational drug use is a punishment for a crime. Therefore, no one can endorse decriminalization unless he agrees that recreational drug users should not be sent to jail or prison. This is the core idea of decriminalization I will employ throughout this book. Decriminalization means that no one will be incarcerated – jailed or imprisoned – merely for using a drug for recreational purposes.

II

Decriminalization only changes punitive state policy toward recreational drug *users*. It is noncommittal about how illicit drugs should be produced or sold. Those who support decriminalization can believe that no one should be allowed to manufacture or distribute illicit drugs. Of course, anyone who favors drug decriminalization is likely to have given thought to how drugs should be bought and sold. Most defenders of decriminalization would probably be unhappy about a policy that punished all producers or distributors of drugs. But decriminalization *itself* implies no position on these issues. Decriminalization says only that users themselves should not be punished. What happens to other participants in the drug trade remains an open question, to be decided only after we are clear about what the criminal justice system should do to recreational users.

Because decriminalization itself says nothing about producers and sellers of drugs used for recreational purposes, we should not regard decriminalization as a comprehensive drug policy. In other words, those who favor decriminalization should not be understood to be proposing a "solution" to our nation's "drug problem." Those who advocate decriminalization may propose any number of imaginative solutions, or believe that the problem has no solution at all. They may (and do) differ greatly among themselves about what an "ideal drug policy" would look like. Their only point of agreement is that punishing drug users is not an acceptable part of a policy that aspires to justice.

The fact that someone can endorse decriminalization while having little to say about drug production and distribution is thought to be a major problem only because we tend to begin our debate by asking the wrong question. Those who favor decriminalization are often pressed to provide the details of a comprehensive drug policy. Would drugs be sold in "state stores" run by the government? Or would drugs be sold by the private sector? Would advertising be allowed? What kind of advertising? These (and myriad other) questions are difficult and important. But someone who believes that our existing policy is unjust need not apologize if he is unable to answer them. Since his claim is that criminalization is unjust – not that some other policy would be more socially beneficial – he need not be embarrassed by his inability to specify all of the details of an optimal drug policy.

The decision to decriminalize use while continuing to criminalize production and sale is hardly an unthinkable combination of policies. Many official reports – such as the Shafer Commission – have made this very recommendation, at least for marijuana. In fact, this combination of policies described the era known as alcohol prohibition in the United States. From 1920 to 1933, the sale of alcohol was prohibited by the criminal law, even though no one was punished simply for drinking. In 1921, Supreme Court Justice Oliver Wendell Holmes publicly toasted his eightieth birthday with champagne by explaining that the Eighteenth Amendment prohibited the manufacture, transportation, and importation of alcohol – not possession or use. Nor was the consumption of alcohol a crime in the home. The fact that this combination of policies is referred to as "alcohol prohibition" demonstrates how misleading terminology can be. Paradoxically, what is widely called *prohibition* in the context of alcohol policy is quite compatible with what I call *decriminalization* in the context of illicit drug policy. In our current era of drug prohibition, it is unthinkable that a Justice of the Supreme Court would publicly tout his use of cocaine. The drug prohibition of today is fundamentally unlike the alcohol prohibition of yesterday. Defenders of decriminalization should be quite receptive to the suggestion that our drug policy should replicate our alcohol policy during the era of prohibition.

If decriminalization would allow drug production and sale to be prohibited, what benefits would it accomplish? Many of the objectives that reformers seek – an elimination of the black market, greater tax revenues and the like – would not be achieved if we continue to punish the production and sale of illicit drugs. Anyone who is attracted to decriminalization for economic reasons is likely to want to remove criminal penalties for production and sale as well as for use. But economic gain is not the best reason to oppose prohibition. Our criminal laws must be just. From this perspective, decriminalization as I have defined it here would represent enormous progress. Since hundreds of thousands of people have been jailed or imprisoned merely for using an illicit drug – unjustly, as I will argue – decriminalization would represent a major improvement in our system of criminal law. This gain in justice would be achieved even if we continue to punish drug sellers and fail to reap economic rewards from decriminalization.

III

Opposition to prohibition does not entail that drug use is approved or condoned by the state. The contrary supposition has been a major obstacle to understanding and endorsing decriminalization. Many people reject decriminalization because they fear it "sends the wrong message" about drug use. According to this train of thought, decriminalization sends the message that drug use is not morally wrongful. It sends the message that we condone recreational drug use.

Perhaps recreational drug use is morally wrongful; perhaps it is not. I will return to this controversial topic in chapter 2. At this time, I point out only that decriminalization itself takes no position on whether drug use is wrongful. We can and do believe that many activities are immoral without resorting to punishment. We can all describe any number of activities – such as breaking contractual promises or lying to friends – that no one proposes to criminalize, even though most everyone agrees that they are wrongful. Similarly, decriminalization does not imply that we condone or approve of recreational drug use. In no other context do we think that the failure to put people in jail indicates that we condone or approve of what they do. To be anti-prohibition is not to be pro-drug.

In case there is any doubt about where the state stands on behavior it does not punish, we should recognize that support for decriminalization is consistent with any number of state mechanisms to discourage drug use. Taxation and education are the most obvious non-criminal devices to change behavior. We can produce less of what we do not want by taxing it heavily or by educating people about its dangers. A host of imaginative strategies to shape behavior are available to the state as well. The ONDCP has encouraged major movie studios as well as individual directors and writers to promote anti-drug messages in their films. The ONDCP has made agreements with Internet search engine companies so that anti-drug advertisements automatically appear on the computer screens of persons who search for terms like "pot" and "weed." As long as these kinds of efforts are made, no one should be tempted to think that the state condones or approves of illicit drug use, even if we become unwilling to resort to criminal punishment.

Again, I suspect that people who reject decriminalization because it "sends the wrong message" are likely to ask the wrong question about drug policy. Suppose, for example, that we already had criminal laws that punished people for breaking their contractual promises or lying to their friends. A plea to repeal these laws would probably be resisted on the grounds that it would suggest that these activities are encouraged or condoned. To my knowledge, however, no one claims that our failure to enact laws to punish people who break their contractual promises or lie to their friends "sends the wrong message." This response is made only when we need a reason not to repeal some law we already have; it is seldom advanced as a reason to enact a new law. From my perspective, however, the basic question that must be answered is why we are justified in continuing to punish recreational drug users. Our concern not to "send the wrong message" provides no more of a reason to retain an unjust law than to enact it in the first place.

Decriminalization, then, is not pro-drug. It may not even be accurate to characterize it as pro-choice. Decriminalization need not imply that the decision to use drugs is personal, so that the state should not try to influence how that decision is made. The state need not be neutral about whether people make good choices. As I will argue in chapter 2, however, the arguments in favor of *punishing* those who do not make good choices turn out to be remarkably weak.

IV

Decriminalization is about state punishment – about how the criminal justice system should respond to recreational drug use. It entails no position about how institutions other than our system of criminal justice should respond to drug use. Institutions can react negatively to those who engage in given kinds of conduct, even though their conduct is not a crime. A variety of responses consistent with decriminalization might be extraordinarily effective in discouraging the use of illicit drugs. Let me mention a few. I do not endorse any of these ideas as desirable; my only point is that they are not ruled out by decriminalization as I define it here.

First, public and private schools might test students for illicit drugs and sanction them in various ways if their tests are positive. Possible sanctions might include not allowing drug users to participate in extracurricular activities. Moreover, public and private employers might test employees for drugs. Employees who use illicit drugs might even be fired. In addition, landlords might be allowed to require tenants to abstain from given drugs specified in a lease, and to evict those who violate their agreements. Clubs like the Rotary Club and organizations like the Boy Scouts need not implement a policy of nondiscrimination against illicit drug users. Needless to say, these examples are not imaginary; 196 of the Fortune 200 companies require pre-employment or random drug tests. Of course, all of these sanctions are precluded by decriminalization if they are modes of punishment. But I do not believe that people are punished when they are barred from extracurricular activities, fired from their jobs, or evicted from their apartments. These consequences are hardships – sometimes more severe than the effects of being thrown into jail – but I do not regard them as kinds of punishments. If I am correct, these kinds of responses are compatible with decriminalization as I understand it.

I need hardly say that decriminalization has no implications for whether individuals will come to regard illicit drug use as fashionable and trendy, or as foolish and reprehensible. The general point should be clear. Decriminalization is not a formula for how society at large must treat illicit drug users. Individuals and institutions might continue to respond negatively to drug use – with one important limitation. Drug users must not be punished by the criminal law.

V

Decriminalization allows the state to criminalize drug use in specific contexts in which it is especially dangerous. Although the criminal law must not punish drug use *per se*, it may punish persons who increase various tangible risks by using drugs. The most familiar example is driving under the influence of drugs that impair judgment or performance. All states prohibit drunk driving, even though no state criminalizes alcohol use itself. In order to be punished, persons must combine drug use with some other activity that is particularly risky. The criminal offense, then, is not drug use itself, but drug use while performing the given activity.

Driving is not the only activity that persons might be punished for performing while under the influence of a drug that impairs judgment or performance. Similar prohibitions would apply to people who operate heavy machinery, fly airplanes, perform surgery, discharge firearms, or the like. These activities are dangerous even when undertaken by persons whose faculties are intact. When judgment or performance is impaired by drug use, these activities become too dangerous to tolerate. Decriminalization would allow persons who perform these dangerous acts to be punished by the criminal law.

There are other ways the criminal law need not be indifferent about drugs, even without punishing drug use itself. One controversial proposal is to treat drug use as an aggravating factor in sentencing persons for non-drug offenses. In other words, burglars and rapists, for example, might be punished more severely if they commit their offenses under the influence of drugs than if they do not. Once again, I do not mention this possibility in order to defend it. Some criminal justice scholars actually endorse the opposite proposal; they contend that drug use should mitigate rather than aggravate the severity of punishment. My only point is that this proposal is compatible with drug decriminalization as I understand it here.

VI

Decriminalization – not punishing recreational drug users – can be brought about in either of two ways. We might distinguish between *de jure* and *de facto* decriminalization. The difference is clear. Under *de jure* decriminalization, all existing crimes of illicit drug use will be repealed. Such offenses would be removed from the books by a deliberate legislative act. Under *de facto* decriminalization, such crimes will not be enforced. They will continue to exist as anachronisms, much like laws prohibiting sodomy or adultery. No one will be arrested, prosecuted, convicted, or punished for violating these laws.

There are reasons to prefer the explicit repeal of crimes of drug use to the alternative of *de facto* criminalization. Laws that still exist can be enforced occasionally and selectively. Even sporadic enforcement of these laws is incompatible with decriminalization. Nonetheless, *de facto* decriminalization would be far easier to implement. Our society does not really know how to conduct a debate about whether a law should be repealed. In fact, very few criminal laws are ever repealed. We readily add new criminal laws to our codes, but rarely remove them. Outdated, discredited criminal laws are much more likely to fall into disuse than to be repealed directly. It is far less politically controversial to simply stop enforcing these laws than to actually require the legislature to remove them from our criminal codes.

The real impact of the criminal law is determined not so much by legislative decisions as by the practices of law enforcement officials – police, prosecutors, and judges. As we have seen, criminal laws against drug use are vigorously enforced, with a devastating effect on the lives of countless individuals. One way to lessen this impact is to call for these crimes to be ignored by law enforcement officials. As long as people are not actually arrested or punished for using drugs, we should not be much concerned about whether this result is achieved through *de jure* or *de facto* decriminalization.

VII

If recreational drug use is decriminalized, what will happen to our current system of making many drugs used for medical purposes available only by prescription? How is this question affected by our inability to decide whether a drug is used medically or recreationally? Will people who presently need a prescription to use a drug for medical purposes be punished if they self-medicate – and somehow obtain that drug without a prescription? These are among the most difficult questions that must be answered in describing a comprehensive blueprint for drug policy reform.

Fortunately, decriminalization itself need not resolve them. It is neutral about the fate of the prescription drug program.

Decriminalization *would* require the abolition of the prescription drug system if it presupposed a particular argument often advanced against prohibition. Many libertarians contend that we have a right to decide what substances to put into our bodies. If we have a right to put a substance into our body for any purpose, we should not need a prescription to be allowed to put a substance into our body for a medical purpose. Libertarians deserve credit for recognizing that principles of justice are at stake in the criminalization debate. I fear, however, that they have misidentified the applicable principle. They often reach the right result, but for the wrong reason. The principle I have presupposed – that punishment must not be imposed in the absence of a compelling justification – is the only principle we need in order to appreciate the injustice of prohibition. Arguments against criminalization need not accept the libertarian claim – that we have a right to decide what substances to put into our bodies.

We should be very reluctant to dismantle the prescription drug system and to allow people to take whatever drugs they want for medical purposes. Even when used correctly, prescription drugs can be extraordinarily dangerous – at least as dangerous as drugs taken for recreational purposes. By some estimates, 100,000 Americans die annually from using prescription drugs. If these drugs became available without the need for a prescription, this toll would almost certainly rise. Billions of dollars would be wasted on ineffective and potentially harmful remedies, and public health would suffer immeasurably. Despite the difficulties of distinguishing recreational from medical use, it is clear that doctors are in the best position to predict whether patients will benefit from taking a drug for medical purposes. Their expertise is essential to decide which substances will be helpful. Recreational drug use, however, is altogether different. Medical expertise is not very helpful in deciding which substances will bring about pleasure or euphoria. Although recreational drug use involves the taking of a drug, it falls largely outside the realm of medical expertise. Therefore, we need not adopt comparable policies toward medical and recreational drug use.

Despite the powerful reasons to retain the prescription drug system, I doubt that we could justify punishing those who lack a prescription but use a drug for a medical purpose. Here again is a possible basis for distinguishing the role of the criminal law in regulating drug use as opposed to drug sale. The criminal law should not punish someone who lacks a prescription but somehow is able to get his hands on a prescription drug. But the criminal law may punish those who *sell* prescription drugs to people without prescriptions. I will not, however, try to defend these positions here. These issues, like many others, show that we can support decriminalization without pretending to have a comprehensive blueprint for a society in which we no longer punish people who use drugs for recreational purposes. Those who oppose prohibition may leave many questions unresolved – including the ultimate fate of the prescription drug system.

VIII

Finally, we can be *selective* about criminalization. To this point, I have mostly supposed that we can debate the reasons for criminalizing "drugs," without further distinctions between the several different kinds of drugs we may want to criminalize. But we might decriminalize the recreational use of some but not all drugs. Because answers to the basic question I have asked depend largely on empirical facts, the case for criminalization should proceed on a drug-by-drug basis. Each drug has different effects on users and on society generally. Clearly, arguments for prohibition are more plausible for some drugs than for others. But we cannot decide which drugs to prohibit without first attending to rationales for criminalization. We must know *what* would count as a good reason to prohibit a drug before we can decide *which* drugs to prohibit.

Our work is not complete when we divide existing drugs into two categories: those we will permit, and those we will prohibit for recreational purposes. We should not be satisfied when we have decided, for example, that caffeine and tobacco should be placed into the former category, while heroin and cocaine should be assigned to the latter category. We need to develop *criteria* for making these classifications. These criteria are needed for two reasons. First, our drug policy must be principled; we need to know *why* we categorize drugs as we do. Second, new drugs will be produced that people will want to use for recreational purposes. These new drugs will have to be assigned to one category or the other. We should not simply assume that all of these drugs must be prohibited. In this vein, consider a warning cast by William Bennett. He cautions: "New illegal products will no doubt continue to appear ... Whichever happens to be the drug of the day, our job is to persist in making it difficult to buy, sell, or use it."[7] But "new" drugs are not "illegal" when they "appear." They only become illegal when legislators decide to prohibit them. Why should we assume that those who use the new "drug of the day" must be punished? Is it really impossible to imagine a new drug that people will want to use recreationally that society should condone and even welcome?

Readers are invited to endorse different policies for different recreational drugs. These different policies can be applied to drugs that already exist, as well as to drugs that are yet to be created. This position is hardly radical; we *already* have very different policies for different recreational drugs. Criminalization has always been selective. We do not punish adult users of alcohol or tobacco, and caffeine is permitted even for children. If we want to proceed cautiously in extending the scope of decriminalization, marijuana is the sensible place to begin. Marijuana is the most widely used and least dangerous illicit drug; the arguments for criminalization I will evaluate in chapter 2 are least plausible when applied here. We could conduct a social experiment by decriminalizing marijuana – perhaps in a single state – before deciding whether to proceed further and decriminalize the use of other drugs. My own preference is more bold – I am not persuaded that we have good enough reasons to punish those who use *any* drug recreationally. We can easily *imagine* a hypothetical drug that we would want to criminalize, but the rationales I will explore do not seem sufficiently compelling to justify criminalizing any drug that actually exists. Of course, I could be mistaken about this sweeping conclusion; the motivations for caution and restraint are easy to understand. Perhaps the arguments to which I now turn will persuade readers that selective prohibition is just after all, and that some but not all recreational drug users should be punished.

2

REASONS FOR CRIMINALIZING DRUG USE

POSSIBLE GOOD ANSWERS

In this chapter I will critically discuss possible *good* answers to the basic question of why persons should be punished for using (some) drugs for recreational purposes – answers that should be taken seriously by anyone who proposes to honestly assess our existing drug policy. I will examine four such answers. I will debate whether recreational drug use should be criminalized in order to protect children, to reduce crime, to safeguard health, or to prevent immorality and a general deterioration of society. I will conclude that none of these possible good answers is nearly good enough. If I am correct, we lack a good reason to punish the hundreds of thousands of persons who have been incarcerated for the crime of using drugs. Punishment is unjust when imposed for inadequate reasons. Therefore, drug prohibition is unjust.

Of course, our drug policy is unjust only if I am correct that the state does not have a good enough reason to punish drug users. My conclusion could be mistaken for any of five distinct reasons, and I must be candid about the potential weaknesses in the structure of my argument. First, the rationales I assess in this chapter might be better than I believe them to be. Many of the empirical facts about drugs I will cite are enormously controversial. Topics like "drugs and crime" are sufficiently complex to merit a lifetime of careful research, and newer and better empirical data become available every week. I do not pretend to have the last word about any of the possible justifications I discuss. *No one* should claim to have the final say on these issues.

Second, we have no precise measure of *how* good a reason must be before it justifies the state in resorting to the drastic step of punishment. We all agree that such reasons must be compelling, but we may disagree about whether a given reason satisfies this criterion. We can appreciate this point by thinking of our drug policy as a war. We have no precise measure of how good a reason must be before it justifies a declaration of war. "Hawks" and "doves" can agree about the reasons for and against waging a war, but disagree about the strength of these reasons. In my judgment, none of the reasons I discuss in this chapter is nearly strong enough to justify a response that is roughly comparable to a war. But reasonable minds may differ.

Third, I might be mistaken in concluding that we lack a sufficient reason to punish recreational drug users because the state may have a good reason I do not examine here. This possibility cannot be dismissed. As I have indicated, no "official" rationale for our drug policy has ever been given. This failure places opponents of our drug policy in a difficult position. We must invent rationales in favor of criminalization before we can begin to evaluate them. When we disagree with a policy, we are tempted to invent bad reasons in its behalf – reasons that are easily refuted. This temptation must be resisted. I hope not to have neglected reasons in favor of our drug policy that are better than the reasons I actually discuss.

Fourth, I may be mistaken to reject our entire drug policy because no single reason shows why we are justified in punishing users of each of the several kinds of illicit drugs that currently exist. Perhaps we have a good reason to punish users of marijuana, a different reason to punish users of cocaine, and yet a third reason to punish users of heroin. If so, each of these drugs should be criminalized, but for different reasons. No one reason justifies the punishment of each and every illicit drug user.

Finally, I may be correct that no single reason is nearly good enough to justify our punitive drug policy, but incorrect to conclude that our policy is unjustified. Reasons that are inadequate when considered individually might combine to form an impressive case overall. Of course, many bad reasons do not equal one good reason. But if each reason has some merit, it may join with other reasons of comparable quality to justify punishing drug users. This point must be kept in mind as we turn our attention to the four subsequent rationales. We must decide not only whether each alone is able to justify criminalization, but also whether each has enough plausibility to combine with others to make a compelling case overall.

Each of the four rationales I will examine is designed to answer what I have called the basic question about our drug policy: Should recreational users of (some) drugs be punished? Should drug use be criminalized? Surely the people who are in the best position to defend our present policy are those who actually believe it to be justified. Generally, we should not trust opponents to identify the best reasons in favor of the very policy they propose to attack. I hope that the arguments of this book will have the effect of stimulating those who support the status quo to explain in greater detail exactly why they are convinced that criminalizing recreational drug use is just. I hope, in other words, that my arguments lead defenders of prohibition to undertake a task they have avoided thus far – to defend prohibition.

Where should we look for possible justifications for criminalization? Since there is no "official" rationale for our drug policy, the most sensible way to proceed is to examine those arguments that have actually been given by the most knowledgeable and thoughtful individuals who have spoken on its behalf. Some of these people are academics who have made their reputations partly by supporting the very criminal laws I challenge here. Others are political appointees who have had the responsibility to oversee and implement drug policy in the United States. The most well-known defenders of our policy include William Bennett, the country's first and most influential "drug czar," and James Q. Wilson, former Chairman of the National Advisory Council for Drug Abuse Prevention and one of the most distinguished and widely respected criminologists in America today.* In addition, I will make frequent reference to the publications of the ONDCP – the official government office charged with establishing policies, priorities, and objectives for drug policy in the United States. Although the ONDCP

---

*In describing people as defenders of drug prohibition, I do not mean to suggest that they have expressed no reservations about the status quo. No one can be enthusiastic about all aspects of existing policy.

has no authority to make law, it is perhaps the best source of an authoritative defense of the law.

DRUGS AND CHILDREN

The first possible answer to the basic question: "Why should recreational users of (some) drugs be punished?" is that prohibition is justified in order to protect children. According to this rationale, the drug war is fought on behalf of America's youth. This rationale has a tremendous appeal. We all want what is best for our children. They need all of the help they can get – for our children are *not* protected from illicit drugs at the present time. According to recent surveys, almost 60 percent of high-school seniors have tried an illicit drug at some point in their lives. Forty-one percent of high-school seniors and 36 percent of sophomores said they had used an illicit drug in the past year. More significantly, almost 33 percent of seniors are "current users" – that is, had used an illicit drug within 30 days of the poll.[8] In light of this alarming statistic, prohibitionists ask us to support whatever policies will prevent children from succumbing to the evils of drugs. This objective seems impossible to achieve unless drug users are punished.

I evaluate this rationale first, but not because it is the most persuasive. Indeed, I think it is probably the *worst* of the four reasons to criminalize drug use that I will evaluate in this chapter. I assess this rationale first because it is so pervasive. Images of children are conspicuous in anti-drug campaigns. According to the ONDCP, the *first* objective of our drug policy is to ensure that America's youth will reject illegal drugs. Needless to say, this objective is thought to require and thereby to justify the punishment of adult drug users.

How should we evaluate this rationale for our existing drug policy? One might be excused for taking it with a large grain of salt. We might assess the sincerity of this rationale by asking whether and to what extent our state is committed to the welfare of children generally. If our government tends to do little to benefit children, it is hard to believe that we would be willing to protect them by undertaking an initiative that costs several billion dollars and incarcerates hundreds of thousands of adults. In fact, our state does much less than other western industrial countries to ensure the health and safety of our children. Millions of kids live in poverty and lack health insurance. Schools tend to be overcrowded and underfunded. If we really were concerned about the welfare of our children generally, we could easily think of several more productive ways to help them than by spending the enormous sums of money we allocate to our punitive drug policy.

Moreover, our alleged concern for the welfare of children seems to vanish as soon as they actually begin to use illicit drugs. When a child is caught with drugs, sympathies are put aside and mercy is seldom forthcoming. The ONDCP promotes "zero tolerance policies for youth regarding the use of illegal drugs." There is a growing trend in criminal justice to prosecute and sentence children as adults. This trend is hard to reconcile with the image of the innocent child who needs to be protected from the dangers of drugs. Against this background, are we really to believe that our deep concern for the welfare of children justifies our policy of punishing drug users?

In addition, our concern to ensure that children remain drug-free is quickly forgotten when doctors purport to detect a syndrome or disorder. Every day in North America, about five million kids take Ritalin, a relatively powerful psychostimulant. The United States and Canada account for about 95 percent of the consumption of Ritalin throughout the world. Many doctors do not believe that "attention deficit disorder" is a genuine medical condition that should be treated with drugs, and denounce Ritalin as nothing more than "cocaine for kids." Of course, adolescents who use real cocaine without a prescription face serious criminal penalties. But the bigger drug problem facing children today probably involves the use and misuse of licit substances.

Despite these skeptical observations, I do not think that this proposed rationale for selective prohibition should be brushed aside or dismissed so casually. Instead, I propose to subject it to a serious evaluation. Might the laudable objective of protecting children really justify the criminalization of drug use? We should begin by asking how this objective *could* justify a policy that imprisons hundreds of thousands of Americans for using drugs.

After all, the vast majority of drug users are adults. How *can* punishing adults help to protect children? The answer would be clear if we believed that adults instigate the behavior we are trying to prevent. In cases in which adults are predators and children are unwilling victims – as in most cases of sexual molestation – we are and ought to be quick to resort to punishment. But drug use is hardly comparable. No one still believes that children reluctantly begin to use drugs because of the pernicious encouragement of adults. The myth of the pusher, for example, has been wholly discredited. We now know that peers – friends and acquaintances, not adult drug dealers – introduce children to illicit drugs. The decision to experiment with illicit drugs like marijuana and ecstasy is not unlike the decision to try licit drugs like tobacco and alcohol. Adult predators or pushers play no significant role here. In any event, adults could be punished in those rare cases in which they *do* encourage children to use drugs. Most jurisdictions already punish such behavior. We could retain these laws, even without prohibiting adult drug use itself.

What, then, *is* the connection between the punishment of adults and the protection of children? Frankly, the matter is unclear. But the most plausible answer, I submit, is as follows. Whenever we treat adolescents differently from adults – and allow adults to do something that we do not allow children to do – we can anticipate what might be called *leakage*. Inevitably, some of what is available to adults will "trickle down" and find its way into the hands of our nation's youth. When we try to prohibit something only for children, kids who are ingenious and determined will somehow succeed in getting it. As long as adults can use something without fear of punishment, we should not expect that children can be effectively prevented from obtaining it. Leakage must be minimized if we really are serious about protecting children from the dangers of drugs. The best way to do so is to prevent adults as well as children from having access to illicit drugs.

The problem of leakage occurs in any context in which we try to protect children but are unwilling to resort to the punishment of adults. Violent depictions or sexual images on television and the Internet are good examples. If we really were serious about preventing leakage – about minimizing the likelihood that children will be exposed to violence or sex – we would ban these pictures for everyone, across the board. That option, however, is intolerable. Instead, we resort to imperfect solutions. We invent devices that scramble cable signals and disable computers from accessing adult sites. We try our best to minimize leakage, without resorting to the extreme device of putting adults in jail for doing what we do not want our children to do.

Leakage is familiar in the context of licit drugs. We have ample evidence of this phenomenon in the case of alcohol and tobacco. Adolescents frequently obtain their supplies of alcohol and tobacco through lawful purchases by adults. Some adults willingly share their supplies with underage drinkers and smokers; other children obtain alcohol or tobacco from adults surreptitiously. If we were as determined to prevent children from using tobacco or alcohol as we are to prevent them from using illicit drugs, we would punish adults who smoke and drink in the way we punish them for using illicit drugs. Of course, we do *not* punish adults who smoke and drink. Despite the anxiety we feel about underage smokers and drinkers, no one seriously proposes that we minimize leakage by resorting to this drastic measure. Instead of punishing adults, we employ other strategies to limit leakage. We take elaborate precautions to restrict direct sales to children, and require purchasers to show proof of age. These safeguards are helpful but flawed; no one pretends they are more than marginally effective. Our measures are easily circumvented, and considerable leakage of licit drugs takes place.

According to the rationale I propose to evaluate here, punishment is justified as a way to prevent the leakage to children that would occur if illicit drug use were decriminalized for adults. I will argue that we have at least four reasons to reject this rationale for criminalization. First, I will contend that this rationale provides a much better reason to punish drug production and sale than to punish use. Second, I will show that we do not effectively prevent leakage, despite our willingness to punish adults. Third, I will maintain that our efforts to reduce leakage often do more harm than good to the very children we are trying to protect. Finally and most controversially, I will argue that the evils of drugs to adolescents are not sufficiently grave to justify the enormous price we pay in trying to prevent leakage.

As a preliminary point, we should reject the use of the word "children" as needlessly inflammatory and misleading. This word suggests that we are talking about policies to protect, say, eight-year-olds. Despite the publicity and concern that surrounds a few notorious cases, not many "children" actually use illicit drugs. In reality, the rationale I examine here involves teenagers – late teens in particular – not pre-teens in elementary schools. Policies that may seem sensible to protect ten-year-olds become far more dubious when applied to college sophomores. Henceforth, I will use the more appropriate term "adolescents" to describe the class of persons we are trying to protect by this rationale for criminalization.

First, this rationale for prohibition would be more plausible if we assume that decriminalization must extend to drug production and sale. Any lawful system of drug distribution might well increase leakage to adolescents. But decriminalization, as I have defined it here, applies only to illicit drug *use*. How would the failure to punish drug users increase leakage? A change in the laws that punish users need not increase supplies of drugs at all. Unless greater supplies of drugs became available, it is hard to see why we should anticipate that greater amounts of drugs would turn up in the hands of kids. *Perhaps* a bit more leakage might occur if we stopped punishing drug users. The failure to punish users might stimulate the demand for drugs; greater demand might lead to an increase in supply, which might facilitate leakage. But this explanation of why decriminalization might cause leakage is far less plausible than a scenario in which we imagine that adolescents are able to break into stores in which decriminalized drugs are lawfully bought and sold. As long as production and sale are prohibited, decriminalization might allow us to prevent leakage as effectively as we do today.

Or, rather, as *ineffectively* as we do today. The next reason to reject this rationale for punishing recreational users of illicit drugs is that it fails to accomplish its goal – prevention of a substantial amount of leakage. Since adults are willing and able to obtain illicit drugs, leakage to adolescents is bound to occur, despite our massive efforts to curtail it. The most telling indication of failure is the availability of illicit drugs, rather than the number of adolescents who succumb to them. In 1999, over 56 percent of adolescents between the ages of twelve and seventeen said that illicit drugs were "easy to obtain." Eighty-nine percent of high-school seniors said that marijuana is "fairly easy" or "very easy" to find. Generally, they report that the difficulty of acquiring illicit drugs is comparable to the difficulty of obtaining alcohol or tobacco – where we do not resort to punishing adults. Prohibitionists tend to respond to these reports by saying that we need to try harder, and to redouble our determination to punish adult users. But more than thirty years of warlike efforts have not proved effective in keeping drugs out of the hands of adolescents who want to get them. Why think that we will succeed tomorrow, when we have failed yesterday and today? Notice that the number of adolescents who report that drugs are easy to obtain is far greater – nearly four times greater – than the number who actually use them regularly. The great majority of adolescents do not use drugs, but not because they cannot find them.

Our punitive policies probably succeed in preventing *some* leakage to adolescents. Admittedly, a number of adolescents did *not* say that illicit drugs were easy to obtain. Drugs may take a bit more time and effort to locate because they are not freely available to adults. We cannot predict how much more leakage would occur if drug use were decriminalized, largely because we do not know exactly how drugs would be produced or distributed under such a system. More importantly, we need to inquire *how much* more leakage would have to take place before we should proclaim criminalization to be justified. Even steadfast supporters of our policy should regard this question as difficult. We sometimes talk as though we should approve of punishment if it succeeds in preventing a single teenager from succumbing to the evils of drugs. Such extreme rhetoric cannot be taken seriously. As I have suggested, we could easily make a far more dramatic improvement in the welfare of adolescents with only a tiny fraction of the resources we allocate to drug prohibition.

How much leakage *do* we prevent? Again, we do not know. Prohibitionists may be encouraged by the substantial decrease in the use of illicit drugs among adolescents over the past twenty years. Although recent statistics about the extent of drug use among adolescents may seem to be alarming, we need to be reminded of the progress that has been made. In 1979, the year of peak drug use in the United States, about 25 million youths were current users of illicit drugs. But these findings do not really provide much basis for believing that our punitive drug policies are successful in preventing significant amounts of leakage. Over the same period of time, the use of alcohol among adolescents has declined as well. In 1979, nearly 50 percent of twelve- to seventeen-year-olds reported drinking at some point in the previous month; now that figure is barely 20 percent. Many factors explain this downward trend in the consumption of alcohol among adolescents. Obviously, however, an increase in our willingness to punish adult drinkers cannot be among these factors. Evidently, substantial reductions in drug use among adolescents can be (and have been) produced without resorting to the extreme measure of incarcerating adults.

We have a third reason to reject this rationale for criminalization. Even if our policy prevents some amount of leakage, this alleged justification for punishing drug users is persuasive only if it achieves a net gain in the welfare of adolescents. No one endorses a cure that is worse than a disease. Parents desperately want what is best for their kids; they want to prevent them from using drugs. As we have seen, however, millions of adolescents stubbornly persist, notwithstanding our efforts. What is best for these kids? We can get a perspective on this question by asking what a parent should be worried about when he suspects or learns that his son or daughter is taking drugs. Two very different kinds of answers might be given. First, the parent might be concerned about the effects of the drugs. Second, he might fear that his son or daughter will be arrested and punished. Which fear is greater? For the vast majority of adolescents who use drugs, the second concern is far more worrisome than the first. As we will see, the effects of drugs on adolescents are likely to be minimal and temporary. But the effects of punishment are often substantial and lasting. The worst thing we can do to adolescents is to turn them into criminals and to punish them. And we *have* been punishing them – at an alarming rate. In 1986, thirty-one of every 100,000 adolescents were incarcerated for drug offenses. By 1996, 122 of every 100,000 were sent to prison for drug offenses – a 391 percent increase. The last thing we should do to adolescents who make minor mistakes is to place them in environments that are likely to exert a negative influence. If we really are concerned about the welfare of the next generation, we should not be eager to punish so many of them.

Dr. Thomas Gleaton, director of the Parents Resource Institute for Drug Education, apparently disagrees with my judgment that the consequences of arrest and punishment are likely to be worse than the effects of drugs themselves. He has said: "If my child, my loved one, or my friend breaks the law by using illicit drugs, please arrest him or her."[9] Fortunately, most parents know better than to follow this bizarre advice. When our sons or daughters use drugs, caring parents have far more to fear from the criminal justice system than from the effects of the drugs. Few parents are so misguided that they go to the police in an effort to protect their adolescents from the dangers of drugs.

Parents who demand that drug users should be imprisoned in order to protect children rarely consider the very real possibility that their own children will be sent to jail as a result of the policies they endorse. Every parent should be made to answer the following question: "Suppose *your* son or daughter is caught using drugs. How much time do you think they should spend in jail?" Many parents naively suppose that criminalization will effectively prevent their kids from using drugs, but seldom think about the justifiability of prohibition when their own teenagers are arrested. We approve of punishing your kids to protect my kids, but feel altogether differently when my kids are punished to protect yours. Some parents have learned this lesson the hard way. The realization that punishment is the more serious danger to adolescents has contributed to the formation of groups like Families Against Mandatory Minimums (FAMM).

How, then, should parents respond when they are less worried about drugs than about the risk that their kids will be arrested? Some of the answers to this question strike many prohibitionists as examples of irresponsible parental behavior. A recent survey indicates that nearly a quarter of all drug-using teenagers in the United States are allowed by their parents to use drugs in their homes. About 5 percent of these teenagers were actually introduced to illicit drugs – nearly always marijuana – by their mothers or fathers. Most pundits reacted to this survey as further evidence of the sorry state of family relations in the United States. Newspapers that reported this story related anecdotes about teenagers who wound up in serious trouble because their parents had permitted them to use drugs. Prohibitionists advise parents to make their children aware in no uncertain terms that illicit drug use is wholly unacceptable and will not be tolerated under any circumstances. But serious research on the phenomenon of illicit drug use within families has not been undertaken. Teenagers who use drugs are introduced to them *somehow* and consume them *somewhere*. Most users first acquire drugs from friends in their neighborhoods and schools. We must ask which source – parents or friends – is more likely to lead first-time users to minimize the problems associated with drugs. Most parents who share drugs insist that their teenagers were bound to try them anyway, and that their kids were "protected" by being allowed to use drugs in their homes. "Protection," of course, is mostly from the police. Are these parents really so irresponsible? Perhaps not. Many researchers contend that teenagers who are introduced to alcohol in the home have fewer drinking-related problems than those who begin to use alcohol elsewhere. The same may be true of illicit drugs. We don't know. But parents are hardly foolish for thinking that law enforcement presents a more serious threat to their sons and daughters than drugs, and that a reasonable strategy to reduce the likelihood of arrest and prosecution is to tolerate the use of drugs in the home.

We want to help our kids, but we don't always know how to do it. One thing we *do* know is that punishing parents who use drugs is very bad for their sons and daughters – the very kids we are trying to protect. Suppose a parent uses drugs, and is not as good a parent as he otherwise might be. Can we seriously believe that the welfare of his family is enhanced if we throw that drug-using parent into jail? Children whose parents are imprisoned are far more likely to become criminals themselves. The terrible effects on kids are especially acute when their mothers are punished. Drug prohibition has made women – and mothers in particular – the fastest growing segment of the prison population. Women now make up about 6 percent of all persons incarcerated – more than twice the rate of 1978. Less than 15 percent of these women were imprisoned for crimes of violence. In any other context, our concern for the welfare of children leads us to try very hard to ensure that families remain intact.

But prohibitionists do not hesitate to tear families apart in the guise of protecting children.

We must travel beyond our country's borders to fully appreciate how our punitive drug policies are more harmful than helpful to children. Columbia has recently been awarded over a billion dollars of military aid from the United Stated in an effort to combat drug trafficking. No one should have any illusions about the impact of "Plan Colombia" on the children of South America. The spraying of cocoa crops has sickened hundreds, and perhaps thousands of Colombian kids. Soldiers in the Colombian army have killed a number of schoolchildren between the ages of eight and ten. Perhaps the deaths of innocent children outside of our country just don't count in our assessment of the justifiability of our drug policies. After all, casualties are inevitable and unavoidable in a war. Children in Columbia must die so that our children can be safe from drugs.

So far, I have argued that prohibition does not prevent much leakage to adolescents, and probably causes them a net balance of harm. If I am correct, we have sufficient reason to reject this alleged justification for punishing drug users. But we have a final reason to reject this rationale as well – a reason that is far more controversial than the preceding three. We must confront the most difficult question raised by this rationale: Is it really so crucial that we protect adolescents from drugs? This objective had better be of supreme importance, or it could not possibly justify a war-like effort that is waged in order to achieve it. We should examine more carefully exactly why we are so intent on trying to keep these substances away from adolescents. How bad *are* drugs for kids?

How should we try to get a handle on this question? Of course, we can always fall back on anecdotes about adolescents – like Sue Miller – whose lives were ruined by drugs. As I hope to have shown, however, we should not formulate our drug policy by generalizing from anecdotes. These tragic stories could be matched with accounts of adolescents who used drugs and became president or served on the Supreme Court. Once we move beyond stories, we need evidence about how drugs typically affect the lives of adolescents who use them. What evidence should we seek?

Longitudinal studies provide the best possible evidence about the effects of drugs on adolescents. These studies track persons who used drugs as adolescents over long periods of time, both before and after their drug-consuming years. Longitudinal studies offer valuable insight into two important issues. First, they provide data about how drugs came to affect the lives of those adults who had used them during their adolescent years. Not surprisingly, these effects vary enormously. The lives of most adults were relatively unaffected; the lives of a small minority were devastated. Second, longitudinal studies offer clues about the differences between these two groups of users. They help to explain why most adults who used drugs during adolescence did not suffer as a result, while others suffered considerably.

What do longitudinal studies reveal about the lives of individuals who took drugs as adolescents? Many more such studies are needed before we can answer this question with confidence. Fortunately (for research purposes), however, tens of millions of Americans who now are middle-aged used illicit drugs throughout their adolescence. How do such persons fare relative to a control group of adults of the same age who did not use drugs? If illicit drug use were really so bad for adolescents, one would expect that those who used them would turn out significantly worse as adults than comparably aged individuals who abstained. But the studies do not confirm this expectation.

In the best such studies, young children are given batteries of tests to identify their psychological health.[10] They are asked the following sorts of questions. Do they believe themselves to be happy? Do they regard themselves as attractive and successful? Are they moody or violent? Are they able to control their temper? These same subjects are tested again and again – usually, in three-year intervals. When they become adolescents, some but not all begin to use illicit drugs. Subjects then are placed in three categories: abstainers, experimenters, or frequent, heavy users. Most adolescents fall into one of the first two categories; few are heavy users. By the time they become young adults, most of these subjects had stopped using illicit drugs – an important point to which I will return. Subjects again are given standard psychological tests of well-being; a number of appropriate questions are added. How frequently have they changed jobs? Or been divorced? How much money do they earn? Have they had trouble paying their bills? Their answers to these (and many other similar) questions are tracked over time.

Longitudinal tests reveal that adults who had experimented with illicit drugs tend to be the best adjusted of the three groups. These individuals score highly on standard tests of psychological health. Adults who had been heavy drug users tend to be the least well-off. Many such individuals are maladjusted and alienated, exhibiting poor impulse control and emotional distress. Adults who had been abstainers tend to fall between the two extremes. Their overall psychological state is better than that of heavy drug users, but worse than that of experimenters. Two conclusions can be drawn. Most importantly, moderate recreational drug use among adolescence is no cause for alarm. This conclusion is absolutely crucial for purposes of evaluating the first rationale for our drug policy. It provides the basis for my claim that a concerned parent should be less worried about how drugs will affect his child than about the possibility of arrest and prosecution. Anyone who proposes to punish adult users in order to prevent leakage to adolescents should be prepared to reconsider this rationale in light of the fact that the great majority of drug-using adolescents do not suffer in the long run.

Of course, a minority of adults who used drugs as adolescents – those whose use is heavy rather than moderate – *do* suffer. If criminalization cannot be defended on behalf of the majority of drug-using adolescents, perhaps it can be justified on behalf of the minority whose lives are negatively affected by their abuse of drugs. Perhaps the best way to prevent immoderate, heavy drug abuse is to deter *all* drug use. To achieve this objective, we should continue to endorse a "zero tolerance" approach that encourages adolescents to "just say no."

But this strategy for preventing drug abuse among adolescents is called into question by the second conclusion that can be drawn from these longitudinal studies. We must try to understand why the majority of adolescents who begin to use drugs do *not* become heavy users and encounter serious problems with drugs. The psychological profiles of children enable us to predict why some of these subjects later succumbed to heavy drug use. Even when young, those who later became heavy users tended to exhibit symptoms of alienation, impulsivity, and distress. In other words, the maladjustment of frequent drug users typically *preceded* their initial act of drug use. Heavy drug use does not cause subsequent problems as much as prior problems cause heavy drug use. Young children who later became moderate drug experimenters were more well-adjusted in the first place. This finding has important implications for policies designed to prevent adolescents from experiencing the difficulties associated with heavy drug abuse. Rather than trying to prevent heavy drug abuse by instructing all kids to abstain, we may be more successful by implementing policies to reduce alienation and maladjustment in young children.

With this finding in mind, recall the story of Sue Miller, originally described in chapter 1. Her fate is typically related to help us appreciate the evils of drugs. But the longitudinal studies I have described help us to resist *pharmacological determinism* – the view that drugs affect us solely as a result of their chemical properties. A moment's reflection shows that pharmacological determinism cannot possibly be true. Those in lower socioeconomic classes are no more likely to try drugs, but are far more likely to develop serious drug problems. The chemical properties of drugs cannot begin to explain why persons with more economic resources are better protected from abuse and addiction. In fact, pharmacological determinism fails to answer most of our crucial questions. We should ask why Sue – unlike the vast majority of adolescents who use drugs – came to develop severe drug problems. Instead of blaming drugs for all of her subsequent difficulties, we might search for something in her past to differentiate her from the great majority of drug-using adolescents who do not become criminals or die from drug abuse.

Of course, those who hope to prevent heavy drug abuse in adolescents are likely to become impatient with this recommendation. We would all like to address "root causes" and to improve the conditions under which our children are raised. But this objective is utopian. What realistic measures can we undertake *now* to minimize the risk that adolescents will become heavy drug users? There is no panacea. Perhaps we can make progress by adopting programs that appear to reduce the incidence of "binge drinking" among students. Many adolescent students drink; a minority of them drink excessively and destructively. Programs designed to educate and warn students about the dangers of overconsumption have not produced encouraging results. A promising alternative – sometimes called the "social-norms" approach – is to inform students of data that shows that binge drinking is less common than they tend to suppose. Students who are inclined to overestimate the extent to which their peers bing drink are more likely to bing drink themselves. Once they appreciate that the phenomenon is not so widespread, they are more inclined to moderate their own consumption. Paradoxically, programs designed to call attention to the severity of the problem are counterproductive, reinforcing stereotypes among students that many of their peers are bing drinkers. Perhaps such findings will prove useful as we try to design more realistic ways to reduce heavy drug abuse among adolescents. I do not, however, purport to "solve" the "drug problem" among either adults or adolescents. My only claim is that highly publicized punishments of moderate drug users do not appear to be an effective means to reduce heavy drug abuse.

Middle-aged adults should not be surprised by my claim that drugs are not nearly as destructive for the vast majority of adolescents as prohibitionists often pretend. They must be aware that the drugs they consumed in their youth did not ruin their lives. Parents who used drugs as adolescents somehow managed to survive the ordeal. Still, these same parents are often persuaded that we should imprison those who do today what they did not so long ago. Why do they believe this? They cannot think that their own lives would have been improved if they had been thrown into jail. Sometimes, they are led to believe that the drugs of today are unlike the drugs they took during their adolescence. The drugs now available are said to be more potent, and therefore more dangerous, than those consumed a generation ago. Most of these claims are demonstrably false. Although some kinds of drugs tend to be somewhat more potent than a generation ago, other kinds of drugs – such as LSD – are less so. And higher potency is not always bad. In the case of marijuana, an increase in potency (measured by higher tetrahydrocannabinol content) might actually prove beneficial. The primary health hazards of marijuana derive from the fact that it is smoked. Risks increase with the quantity, rather than with the potency of what is smoked. The greater the potency, the less that is needed to reach the same psychological state. The same is true of heroin. Higher potencies have contributed to the recent trend of smoking rather than injecting heroin, which minimizes the risks of AIDS and hepatitis – health hazards far greater than the effects of heroin itself. Anyone who worries about illicit drugs because of the risks to health need not always be alarmed by increases in potency.

In reflecting on this rationale for criminalization, we should be aware of our long history of believing exaggerated accounts of the dangers of drugs for adolescents. We all remember stories about how cigarettes were alleged to stunt the growth of kids. Many subsequent stories turned out to be no less mythical. The abuse of the drug war to protect children probably reached its zenith in the hysteria over "crack babies" that began in the mid-1980s. Newspapers, magazines, and television collaborated to portray the devastating effects suffered by newborn infants whose mothers smoked crack during their pregnancies. Some doctors predicted that crack babies would have to be written off as a "lost generation" or a "biological underclass." These fears were used to criminalize the use of crack during pregnancy as a form of child abuse, and to forcibly remove infants from their drug-using mothers. Today, few researchers believe that cocaine does more harm to fetuses than cigarettes. Studies find no major differences between infants who had and had not been exposed to cocaine *in utero*. One exhaustive recent study concludes "the data are not persuasive that *in utero* exposure to cocaine has major adverse developmental consequences in early childhood ... These harms are unlikely to be of the magnitude of those associated with *in utero* exposure to the legal drugs tobacco and alcohol."[11] Moreover, early intervention helps to reverse any damage that may have occurred. Despite these findings, some women who used cocaine during their pregnancy were convicted of murder in 2001 (especially in South Carolina) when their children were stillborn. Everyone wants what is best for newborns. But no one seriously proposes that infants whose mothers consumed alcohol or smoked cigarettes (or failed to seek prenatal care, or ate deficient diets) should be forcibly removed from their mothers – who should then be imprisoned – because these women did not behave in optimal ways during pregnancy. Exaggerated fears about the dangers of illicit drugs provide a poor reason to tear families apart and throw women into jail.

I do not pretend that the foregoing observations will put to rest all of our fears about drugs and kids. These anxieties will always be with us. Adolescents will continue to engage in behaviors that alarm their parents. They stay up late, eat junk foods, have sex (frequently unprotected), study too little, skip school, play extreme sports, incur too much debt, and the like. The extent of these risks should not be exaggerated. We must be sufficiently mature and honest to admit that some problems will never be completely solved. In any event, our punitive drug policies cannot possibly be justified in order to protect our sons and daughters from the evils of drugs. In no other context would we approve of a policy that prevents adults from engaging in a type of activity simply because it is bad for children. This rationale for criminalization treats adults as though they were children. I have argued that punishing adults for this purpose is ineffective and causes great harm to those it purports to protect. Finally, I have suggested that drug use, even among adolescents, does not appear to be sufficiently destructive to justify the punishment of adults in our futile effort to prevent it.

DRUGS AND CRIME

Rates of violent crime in the United States are unacceptably high. Still, enormous progress has been made. The country experienced a significant reduction in crime in the 1990s. Experts disagree about why. Possible answers include overall economic prosperity, an aging population with fewer adolescents, better police work, longer sentences for violent criminals, more effective precautions by citizens and the private sector, and even the availability of safe and legal abortions (which prevented unwanted children who might have become criminals from being born). Another possible answer is the strict enforcement of laws that punish drug users. "Drug control is crime control," proclaimed Rudolph Giuliani, former mayor of New York City. The goal of reducing violent crime provides the second of the four possible answers to the basic question I will evaluate in this chapter. According to the ONDCP, the most important objective of our drug policy – after the protection of children – is to "increase the safety of America's citizens by substantially reducing drug-related crime and violence." In this section, I will critically respond to the rationale that crime prevention justifies our policy of punishing people who use illicit drugs for recreational purposes.

Many knowledgeable critics of this rationale would be quick to contest it on empirical grounds. Our willingness to punish illicit drug users may do little to explain the recent decline in rates of violent crime. Whether increases in the punishment of drug users coincide with decreases in violent crime depends on the year we choose as the baseline of comparison. In the 1990s, crime plummeted while punishments for drug use soared. Suppose, however, that we adopt a somewhat longer perspective, and examine these phenomena since 1980. Our prison population has tripled since 1980 – much of which, as we have seen, is due to greater punishments for drug users. Yet we now have about the same level of non-drug crime as we had then. If the punishment of drug users really were an effective means to reduce violent crime, one would expect that an increase in the former would be correlated more closely with a decrease in the latter over long periods of time.

Moreover, we should insist on getting the correct statistics before confidently proclaiming that drug use causes crime. Prohibitionists often point out that a high percentage of criminals test positive for illicit drugs. What should we conclude from this fact? The percentage of criminals who are drug users is not as meaningful as the percentage of drug users who are criminals. The latter percentage, after all, is extraordinarily low. Those who believe that drug use causes crime must struggle to explain why the vast majority of drug users never engage in criminal conduct.

Empirical misgivings aside, I am more interested in assessing whether this rationale is acceptable from the perspective of justice. In a just state, *should* we allow drug users to be punished in order to reduce violent crime? Initially, we might be tempted to answer affirmatively. In principle, crime-reduction is probably the *best* rationale for punishing illicit drug users. Everyone understands the importance of reducing violent crime. Many criminal laws that almost certainly are justified – those that punish solicitation, for example – are designed to prevent serious crime *before* it happens. Laws prohibiting drug use might be justified if they serve this same purpose. If we really succeed in preventing significant amounts of crime by punishing illicit drug users, how could any reasonable person believe that such punishments are not justified?

To evaluate this rationale, we must look more carefully at *how* and *why* the punishment of recreational drug users might be thought to reduce violent crime. In other words, we must try to understand the nature of the *drug–crime connection*. This topic is extraordinarily complex. Fortunately, social scientists have developed very powerful frameworks for understanding the link between drugs and crime.[12] At least three types of crimes might be linked to drug use. The first types of crimes are *systemic*. Systemic crimes are those that occur because drug use is illegal and illicit drugs are bought and sold in black markets. When something goes wrong with illicit drug production or sale, buyers and sellers do not have the redress that we take for granted when a problem arises with a lawful product. If a seller cheats a buyer, or if a consumer refuses to pay a dealer, or if a user is disappointed, the complaining party can hardly go to the courthouse to file a lawsuit. Disputes of this sort must be resolved outside of normal legal channels. As a result, one would expect that illicit drug markets would be violent. Our history appears to confirm this expectation. Black markets were notoriously violent throughout the era of alcohol prohibition. Today, the black market in cocaine is comparable. The systemic crimes associated with illicit drugs include highly publicized cases of murder due to disputes involving illegal drug transactions. Sometimes, innocent children are killed in gun battles between rival drug gangs. These tragedies always give rise to calls for stricter enforcement of existing drug laws. Paradoxically, stricter enforcement can make dealing more profitable, and thereby increase the violence and incidence of the very systemic crimes it is designed to prevent.

Without question, much of the violent crime associated with illicit drugs is systemic. By most estimates, this category accounts for about 75 percent of drug-related crime. In 1988 in New York City, as many as 85 percent of crack-related crimes were caused by the market culture associated with crack sales, primarily territorial disputes between rival dealers. Decriminalization would reduce the incidence of these systemic crimes. Of course, systemic crime would be *drastically* reduced if decriminalization were extended beyond drug use to include drug production and sale. Because these systemic crimes would be decreased, even opponents of decriminalization do not always predict that it would lead to a net increase in crime. Despite his enthusiasm for prohibition, James Q. Wilson writes: "It is not clear that enforcing the laws against drug use would reduce crime. On the contrary, crime may be caused by such enforcement."[13] According to this school of thought, an overall increase in crime is the price we must be willing to pay for the several advantages we gain by laws that prohibit drug use.

In my judgment, Wilson is half right and half wrong. He is probably correct to think that more crime, rather than less, is caused by our prohibition of drug use. He is incorrect, however, to conclude that the advantage that such laws allegedly produce – a significant decrease in the incidence of drug use – outweighs the disadvantage he cites. I believe that the enormous amount of systemic crime caused by prohibition is too high a price to pay for any of the speculative goods that might result from punishing drug users. Unfortunately, I cannot prove that I am correct about how these advantages and disadvantages should be balanced – a point to which I will return in chapter 3. But I would bet that the innocent victims of systemic crimes would tend to agree with my assessment that the drawbacks outweigh the benefits. The mother of a teenage drug user killed in a confrontation with police would be stunned to learn that serious academics concede that decriminalization would have saved the life of her child, but oppose it nonetheless.

Before leaving the topic, I must point out that the phenomenon of systemic crime associated with the illicit drug trade is much more complex than appearances might suggest. First, not all black markets are especially violent. Many black markets exist in America other than illicit drug markets – such as those involving gambling. These other black markets are not notorious for their high rates of violence. Second, even black markets in drugs are not particularly violent in other countries. In Australia, for example, significantly less systemic violence is associated with drug transactions – even though rates of drug use are roughly comparable to those in the United States. Finally, much of the violence in America's illicit drug trade appears to be attributable to predispositions toward violent lifestyles that predate involvement with drugs. In other words, drug markets may not cause violence as much as attract people who were already prepared to be violent. Therefore, not all of the violence associated with the drug trade should be attributed to the fact that drug transactions are illegal. Factors peculiar to contemporary America explain this violence. When an innocent child is killed in a drive-by shooting between rival dealers, we are quick to blame the drugs, but reluctant to mention other factors – most notably, guns. These violent acts might just as well be attributed to America's "gun culture" as to our "drug culture."

Whatever the deep explanation of the systemic violence associated with illicit drugs in the United States, we must recognize that decriminalization would reduce this category of crime. This recognition puts us in a better position to decide whether selective prohibition can be justified as a means to prevent crime. The disputed and crucial issue is not simply whether drug use causes crime, but whether drug use causes criminal conduct that would persist even if drug use itself were not prohibited. When we try to assess the merits of decriminalization by analyzing the drug–crime connection, we should remember that most criminal behavior associated with drugs is not caused by drugs *per se*, but rather by the fact that drug use is illegal.

This crucial point must be kept in mind as we turn our attention to the second type of crime associated with illicit drugs: *economic* crime. Drug use causes economic crime for a simple reason. Partly because of addiction, illicit drug users tend to want drugs very badly, and are willing to go to extraordinary lengths to obtain them. Many illicit drugs are expensive. This combination of strong demand and high price leads users to commit economic crimes to get the money to buy drugs. Some estimates of the number of property offenses committed by drug users are astronomical. A few experts once conjectured that virtually *all* of the economic crime in New York City was committed by heroin addicts who needed to finance their habits. Other experts replied that these estimates were wild exaggerations. Who is correct? One way to estimate the extent of economic crime committed by addicts who need money to finance their habits is to survey prison inmates convicted of economic crimes. Only about 25 percent of adult inmates who use illicit drugs and commit economic crimes cite their drug use as a primary motivation for becoming involved in criminal activity. Many such persons began committing economic crimes prior to using drugs. Even William Bennett, in arguing against "drug legalization," admits that "many drug-related felonies are committed by people involved in crime *before* they started taking drugs."[14]

Whatever the true extent of economic crime associated with illicit drugs, we must struggle to determine whether such crime is caused by drugs, or is caused by drug prohibitions. If less economic crime would occur under decriminalization than prohibition, the goal of reducing economic crime could hardly be the rationale for punishing drug users. Unfortunately, this question is not easy to answer. Again, the main difficulty is our lack of certainty about how illicit drugs would be bought and sold if drug users were no longer punished. Under most models of decriminalized markets, illicit drugs would be far less expensive. Some academics have estimated that heroin could be lawfully bought and sold at about 2 percent of its current, black-market price. If this estimate were roughly accurate, one would anticipate that decriminalizing the sale of heroin (and other illicit drugs) would cause a drastic reduction in economic crime. This prediction is based partly on an examination of the extent of economic crime associated with licit drugs. Alcoholics and tobacco addicts rarely steal to purchase their drugs, but not because their addictions are less powerful – but because they can afford to buy what users of illicit drugs cannot.

On the other hand, as I will explain in more detail in chapter 3, drugs in decriminalized markets may *not* be significantly less expensive. The price of these drugs would depend on unknown variables like the rate of taxation. In addition, if decriminalized drugs really were less expensive, greater numbers of people might be inclined to use them. Greater numbers of users might translate into a higher population of addicts, who in turn might cause greater amounts of economic crime – even though drugs were cheaper. No one should be very confident about how the incidence of economic crime would be affected by the decriminalization of drug use. Despite this uncertainty, one point is clear. The incidence of economic crime associated with illicit drugs is not simply attributable to illicit drugs *per se*, but to complex features of drug markets – most notably, to the high price of drugs. High prices are due more to the fact that drug sales are illegal than to the cost of producing illicit drugs. If our objective is the reduction of economic crime, we are better off controlling markets and fixing the price of illicit drugs at the point at which the incidence of economic crime is minimized. There is no reason to believe that this optimal point corresponds to the cost of drugs in the black markets of today. We should be very reluctant to believe that punishing drug users is an effective way to reduce economic crime.

The third type of crime in the drug–crime connection is *psychopharmacological*. This category of crime results from the effects of drugs themselves, rather than from the fact that their use and sale is prohibited. The use of drugs may cause violent, criminal acts in somewhat different ways. Drugs may release inhibitions that can generally be restrained. Drugs may impair judgment and perception, leading users to act in ways they would otherwise avoid. According to William Bennett, "the fact is that under the influence of drugs, normal people do not act normally, and abnormal people behave in chilling and horrible ways."[15] This account of the connection between drug use and crime is reminiscent of the story of Dr Jekyll and Mr Hyde. Dr Jekyll consumed a potion that transformed him into the homicidal Mr Hyde. The psychopharmacological effects of this potion caused an otherwise law-abiding physician to become a violent monster. Of course, this story is purely fictitious. If any existing drug resembled the potion in this story, we would have excellent reasons to criminalize its use.

Fortunately, no existing drug resembles this fictional potion. Scholars are far more ambivalent than Bennett about this explanation of the drug–crime connection. Of course, we can always fall back on anecdotes. But research provides no evidence that people under the influence of marijuana or heroin are more likely to become aggressive and violent. These drugs tend to have the opposite effect; their psychopharmacological properties cause users to become passive. Studies indicate that users of marijuana are substantially under-represented among violent criminals when researchers are careful to control for other variables such as age. The situation with cocaine is a bit less clear. Cocaine users themselves, however, report that the drug almost never leads them to commit violent acts they would not have performed otherwise. Ironically, alcohol is the drug most likely to lead to psychopharmacological crime. If we accept this rationale for pun-ishing drug users – and prohibit drugs that cause people to become violent and aggressive – we would begin by punishing drinkers. More generally, if we propose to ban those drugs that are implicated in criminal behavior, no drug would be a better candidate for criminalization than alcohol. In 1998, the National Center on Addiction and Substance Abuse (NCASA) reported that 21 percent of persons in state jails or prisons for violent crime were under the influence of alcohol and no other drug at the time they committed their crime. Only 3 percent were under the influ-ence of cocaine or crack alone, and 1 percent were under the influence of heroin alone.

Alcohol aside, we cannot justify the punishment of drug users in order to prevent either systemic, economic, or psychopharmacological crime. Might some other explanation show how punishing drug users could reduce crime? Another possible connection between drugs and crime involves the well-known "broken windows" hypothesis. According to this hypothesis, street life in a community has an indirect effect on violent crime rates. Minor disorder breeds major disorder, since it leads people to believe that neighborhoods are out of control and no one cares. Major disorder causes fear and retreat by law-abiding citizens, which in turn gives rise to greater amounts of criminality. This hypothesis supports the belief that serious crime can be reduced by arresting even petty drug offenders.

Does this hypothesis provide the key to a rationale for criminalization? I think not. Our basic question – Should drug use be criminalized? – asks for a good reason to punish drug users. The "broken windows" hypothesis does not answer *this* question; it presupposes that drug use is *already* a crime. This is the very supposition we are challenging. We need a reason to believe that laws against drug use should exist, not a reason to enforce laws that exist already. Once decriminalized, illicit drug use need be no more analogous to a "broken window" than the use of tobacco. There is histori-cal precedent for this view of illicit drug use. In Victorian England, for example, the use of opiates was as much a part of society as the drinking of alcohol or the smoking of tobacco. Admittedly, tolerance of the disorder-liness associated with *public* drug use might be analogous to a failure to fix broken windows. But we can prohibit public disorderliness without criminalizing drug use generally. At best, the "broken windows" hypothesis provides a reason to enforce existing laws, even when the offenses seem minor and trivial. It does not give us a justification for creating criminal offenses in the first place.

We must explore a final possible connection between drugs and crime. Perhaps the rationale for criminalizing drug use is similar to the rationale for criminalizing vagrancy. We reduce crime by punishing vagrants because of the statistical overlap between those who are vagrants and those who are criminals. Punishing illicit drug users is likely to reduce crime for the same reason – because of the statistical overlap between those who use illicit drugs and those who commit crimes. Criminals are likely to be young males. Coincidentally, illicit drug users are likely to be young males as well. The overlap between these two groups is not wholly coincidental, since young males who use illicit drugs have indicated their willingness to break laws and defy authority. By imprisoning large numbers of drug users, we prevent significant numbers of crimes that many of these users would have perpetrated.

This rationale for punishing drug users and vagrants – as well as the need to fix broken windows – is clearly more compelling in lower-class neighborhoods. The statistical overlap between drug use and criminality is greater when drug users are poor. Why? Clearly, the answer has nothing to do with the psychopharmacological effects of drugs. Instead, drugs correlate with criminality when used by people who have the kinds of problems associated with poverty. Drug use – like other consensual crimes such as gambling and prostitution – can push people over a cliff. Whether an activity will push someone over a cliff depends on how close he was to the edge in the first place. People with greater financial and social resources have a wider safety net. Disaster is only a short distance away for those who live at the social and economic margins of society. Such people are more likely to resort to criminality to solve whatever problems precede or are exacerbated by their use of drugs.

This final account may offer the most plausible explanation of why crime might be reduced by punishing drug users. To be sure, this explanation has been challenged on empirical grounds. A growing numbers of scholars believe that punishing drug use actually causes more crime in lower-class neighborhoods than it prevents. Some of the reasons for this belief are controversial; I will return to them in chapter 3. Here, I simply point out that incarcerated drug users will have to be released and returned to their communities *sometime*. Although the Supreme Court has ruled that lifetime imprisonment is not an unconstitutionally severe sentence for the crime of cocaine possession,[16] no one really proposes to keep drug users behind bars indefinitely. Because of the long sentences imposed on them, drug users who are released are less likely to find employment, housing, or to re-establish ties with families. As a result, they are more likely to resort to criminality – and not merely crimes involving drugs. Nearly one-fifth of all persons locked up for nonviolent offenses are eventually rearrested for violent offenses. Although criminalization can produce short-term benefits, it may cause an increase in crime in the long run.

In the remainder of this section, however, I will concede that punishing drug users in lower-class neighborhoods is an effective way to reduce crime. The issue is whether this concession can *justify* criminalization. Does it give us a good reason to believe that justice allows drug users to be punished? We should all have serious reservations before we accept this rationale. We should be reluctant to punish an activity that leads people to fall off a cliff when the main problem is their proximity to the edge. The long-term solution is to move farther from the cliff. Still, we need a short-term solution – a strategy to pursue while we figure out how to achieve the utopian goal of eliminating poverty. In the meantime, can we possibly be justified in punishing drug users as a means to reduce crime?

Two alternatives emerge when we scrutinize this rationale more carefully. First, we might enact criminal laws against drug use solely in lower-class neighborhoods, where the correlation between drug use and criminality is fairly high. Of course, no one explicitly endorses this idea. We appear to be racist and discriminatory when we enforce drug prohibitions in poor but not in middle and upper-class neighborhoods. We cannot blame people for growing up in the wrong social class; the law cannot prohibit the poor from doing what we tolerate among the wealthy. Suppose, then, we enact criminal laws against drug use altogether, for rich and poor alike. This second alternative is objectionable as well. The correlation between drug use and criminality is not especially high in middle- and upper-class neighborhoods. If we choose this option, we will punish conduct in all neighborhoods because of the problems it causes in lower-class communities. This approach casts the criminal net far too widely; it makes criminals of the many in the hope of preventing the misdeeds of the few. About 80 or 90 million living Americans have used illicit drugs; almost 15 million did so last month. No one can seriously believe that we are justified in punishing each of them in order to prevent the offenses that a small fraction would commit. Neither of these two alternatives is palatable.

The "compromise" between these two objectionable alternatives – which closely corresponds to reality – is to *enact* criminal laws against drug use for everyone, regardless of social class – but to *enforce* these laws much more vigorously in poor, minority communities. As a strategy to prevent crime, this compromise makes perfect sense. It is, however, closely analogous to the widely discredited policy of "racial profiling." Since blacks are statistically more likely to commit crimes than whites, we prevent more crimes by arresting blacks than by arresting whites. Of course, the state cannot arrest anyone until he is thought to have committed an offense. The crime of drug use provides the ideal opportunity to make arrests that are designed to prevent the occurrence of more serious crimes.

The foregoing comparisons with vagrancy laws and practices of racial profiling allow us to appreciate the injustice of this rationale for selective prohibition: It fails to provide what I have called a *personal* justification for punishing drug users. We are not justified in punishing someone simply because he is a member of a class of persons in which the incidence of criminality is high. This rationale does not punish individuals because they deserve to be punished for what they have done, but because they are members of a class of people whose tendency to commit crimes is greater than in the general population. Punishing all drug users – or all vagrants or minorities – because a fraction of them will commit crimes is an impersonal justification for punishment.

This point is easily misunderstood. Of course, the criminal law is and ought to be in the business of protecting citizens from the risk of harm. This is why we criminalize drunk driving, for example. Obviously, only a small percentage of drunk drivers actually cause a crash. Still, drunk driving is properly criminalized because it increases the risk of a crash. Isn't the rationale for drug prohibitions comparable? Even though most drug users do not actually commit crimes, isn't drug use properly criminalized because it increases the risk of crime? The two examples are superficially similar, but differ in a crucial respect. In the case of drunk driving, intoxication itself makes driving more dangerous. Drinking impairs the judgment and reflexes of rich and poor alike, directly increasing the risk of an accident. The link between drug use and crime is not comparable. Drug use itself does not increase the likelihood of crime in the way that intoxication increases the likelihood of a crash. Except for the unusual category of psychopharmacological crime in cases like Dr Jekyll and Mr Hyde, the link between drug use and crime is much less direct, and differs from one social class to another. The kinds of people who use drugs may be the same kinds of people who commit crimes, but the drugs they take do not somehow make them commit crimes. Comparable statistical links exist between age and crime, race and crime, gender and crime, and licit drug use and crime. But no one thinks that we are justified in punishing adolescents, minorities, males or drinkers because they pose increased risks of violence. Why not? The answer is straightforward. These people do not deserve to be punished for what they have done. Punishment in such cases would violate the principle that a justification for criminalization must be personal.

I conclude that no account of the drug–crime connection provides an acceptable justification for criminalization. Because of systemic and economic crime, drug prohibition may actually cause more crime than it prevents. And even if the statistical overlap between drug use and violent criminality indicates that we could prevent some of the latter by punishing all of the former, justice would not allow us to do so.

Drugs and health

When anti-drug messages are not aimed specifically at adolescents, they typically emphasize how drugs are bad for those who use them – bad for adults as well as for children. Drugs are bad both physically and psychologically; they harm our bodies as well as our minds. Recall, for example, the famous anti-drug advertisements likening brains on drugs to eggs in frypans. Protecting our physical and mental health is one of the most important functions of the state. Might this objective justify the punishment of persons who use (some) drugs for recreational purposes? Can the protection of health and well-being be the rationale for criminalization?

Few prohibitionists adopt this rationale explicitly. No one seems willing to say: "The state is justified in punishing drug users because illicit drugs are bad for our health." Clearly, however, this rationale is endorsed implicitly. Anyone who proposes that the use of a given drug should be decriminalized is certain to be informed of some study that allegedly shows the drug to pose risks to the health of users. A plea to decriminalize the use of ecstasy, for example, is bound to give rise to the rejoinder that ecstasy is unsafe. This rejoinder may be a perfectly good answer to the question "Should I use ecstasy?" But how is it responsive to our basic question about criminalization? This rejoinder would be irrelevant unless those who support the status quo believe that the goal of protecting health provides a good reason to punish drug users.

How should we begin to evaluate this possible rationale for drug prohibition? Two points are fairly clear. First, we should concede that drugs *are* often bad for the health of those who use them. More precisely, illicit drugs pose *risks* to physical and psychological well-being. Of course, these risks vary in degree from one drug to another. Moreover, the extent of these risks is controversial – a point to which I will return. Still, anyone who wants to minimize health risks should be advised not to use drugs for recreational purposes.

The second clear point is that this objective provides a very strange rationale for drug prohibition. Although the state has a central role in protecting the health of its citizens, it does not ordinarily perform this function by punishing the very persons whose health it endeavors to protect. The FDA, for example, provides a valuable service by ensuring that consumers do not get sick by eating spoiled meat. Criminal penalties can be imposed on sellers of adulterated foods. But no one has ever proposed to put people in jail for eating foods they know to be unhealthy. The idea that people should be punished for taking risks to their health is extraordinary – and very hard to accept in a state in which the scope of the criminal law is limited.

Moreover, this rationale – like the goal of protecting children – is at odds with other policies in the United States. If the improvement of public health were really our objective, we surely could invest our money far more wisely than by funding a massive drug war. Millions of Americans – unlike citizens in other western industrialized states – lack health insurance. Uninsured Americans are disproportionately represented among illicit drug users. Those uninsured individuals who are punished for using illicit drugs cannot be blamed if they do not take this rationale for criminalization seriously. They are entitled to scoff at the idea that the state cares so much about their health that they are punished in order to prevent them from jeopardizing it.

Prohibitionists themselves must recognize this rationale to be implausible, since they tend to endorse it with reservations. When challenged about whether this objective *really* provides the justification for criminalization, they often emphasize not only the importance of protecting the health of the individual, but also the public expense incurred when people make unhealthy choices. Risky behavior raises insurance premiums for everyone, and places a financial burden on health services provided by the state at taxpayer expense. The fact that the cost to the taxpaying public is mentioned so frequently shows how uncomfortable prohibitionists are with the principle that people should be thrown into jail in order to protect their health. In any event, this new consideration does little to improve the plausibility of the rationale. The principle that people should be punished in order to reduce insurance premiums and conserve public resources is not much more credible than the original rationale it is designed to supplement or replace. This principle proves far too much. If applied consistently, it would authorize the criminalization of *any* activity that burdened state health resources.

Beyond these two clear points, the issue becomes murky. We might clarify the issue by inquiring *how* criminalization could succeed in improving health. Two accounts might be defended. First, the infliction of punishment might deter current drug users from persisting in their unhealthy behavior. Drug users might be "scared straight" by the shock of punishment or coerced into treatment, thereby avoiding further deterioration of their health and well-being. Second, the threat of punishment might deter those who do not use drugs from starting to use them. Prospective users who never start will not risk the physical and psychological hazards of drug use.

Neither of these two accounts seems likely to improve health and well-being. Consider the first. This account supposes that the health of drug users will improve (or not deteriorate further) if they are sent to prison. One difficulty with this account is that it assumes that prisoners will stop using drugs. Recent surveys indicate, however, that about 10 percent of all prisoners use illicit drugs while incarcerated. The real difficulty with this account, however, is more fundamental. Prison is obviously deleterious to health – far more deleterious than drugs. We could easily *imagine* a drug that is so detrimental to health that nearly anything that could be done to prevent people from continuing to use it would promote their safety in the long run. Someone might be better off in jail than free to take a drug that killed significant numbers of those who persist in using it. Fortunately, no existing recreational drug is nearly so destructive – with the possible exception of tobacco.

Arguably, the state interest in deterring people from behavior that poses substantial risks to their health and well-being might be sufficiently strong to justify the infliction of criminal penalties – but only when the risks are great and punishments are not severe. Consider, for example, laws requiring drivers of cars to wear seat belts. Of course, these laws are controversial and unpopular. Yet they are far easier to justify than laws prohibiting the use of recreational drugs (when these laws are construed to protect health). The penalty for violating seat-belt laws is minimal; usually, only a small fine is imposed. Since sanctions are so trivial, a case can be made that these laws really do serve the interest of those they punish. Enforcement increases (by a small amount) the likelihood that drivers will buckle their seat belts and survive a crash. Payment of a fine is a minor hardship if it succeeds in decreasing a substantial risk to safety. But it is hard to argue that laws prohibiting the use of recreational drugs are actually in the interest of the very people they punish. The penalties imposed on offenders are too severe to make this claim plausible. As sanctions increase in severity, the "cure" of punishment becomes worse than the "disease" – the risk to well-being that the law is designed to prevent.

The second account of how prohibition might succeed in protecting public health is somewhat more credible. Health will be enhanced if the threat of punishment deters people who do not use drugs from beginning to do so. This account, of course, depends on three assumptions – two of which will be discussed more fully in chapter 3. First, health will not be protected unless criminalization is a reasonably effective deterrent. If the threat of punishment does not dissuade people from experimenting with drugs, no health gains can be achieved. Since about 15 million Americans use illicit drugs each month, the deterrent efficacy of prohibition would appear to be weak. Second, the health of those who *are* deterred from experimentation will be preserved only if they do not substitute more or equally dangerous drugs for those they forgo. We should not assume that those who would use illicit drugs but for the threat of criminal penalties will choose to eat vegetables and fruit rather than to consume some other unhealthy substance. We will return to these two assumptions when we examine a world in which recreational drug use has been decriminalized.

At this juncture, I want to focus on a third assumption that is obviously crucial to any account of how health might be improved by the prohibition of recreational drug use. We cannot fully assess the plausibility of this rationale unless we understand *how* risky drugs really are. If these risks are small, we would hardly be justified in waging a war in order to prevent them. But if these risks are substantial, we are on firmer ground when we take drastic steps to deter drug use. We tolerate seat-belt laws not only because fines are modest, but also because they have been proved to reduce a risk that actually kills some 40,000 drivers and passengers in cars each year. Seat belts have also been shown to be effective in reducing the severity of hundreds of thousands of non-fatal injuries. What are the comparable figures for drug use? Before we are led to punish drug users to protect their health, we should demand convincing evidence that the drugs we prohibit are unhealthy. Where is this evidence? Again, we should not be persuaded by anecdotes – stories of people who swear that their health has been ruined by drugs. We could match these anecdotes with colorful accounts of aged individuals who attribute their longevity to their daily consumption of tobacco and alcohol. Nor should we be persuaded by studies that indicate that users of a given drug "might" encounter "some" risk. We must ask: How great a risk, and what is the probability of its occurrence? A complete response to this possible rationale for selective prohibition must endeavor to assess the extent of health risks caused by the use of illicit drugs.

Epidemiological studies are the easiest and most obvious way to identify the health hazards of any substance – tobacco, for example. If tobacco causes cancer, one would expect that the cancer rates of smokers would be substantially higher than those of non-smokers. Someone who maintains that tobacco causes cancer would be embarrassed if smokers and non-smokers were equally likely to get cancer. Of course, these studies confirm our worst fears about tobacco. What do epidemiological studies tend to show about the effects of illicit drugs?

If we divide the population into two groups – those who have used illicit drugs and those who have not – no existing data show the former to be less healthy than the latter. From a health perspective, the 80 or 90 million Americans above the age of twelve who have used illicit drugs are not readily distinguishable from the somewhat greater number of Americans who have abstained throughout their lifetimes. But two important qualifications are needed. First, existing studies are less helpful in revealing *long-term* risks to health. Few in the United States used illicit drugs prior to the mid-1960s. The incidence of illicit drug use peaked about 1979, when about 14 percent of the population took drugs on a weekly basis. Those who consumed the greatest amounts of drugs in those years were mostly between the ages of forty and fifty at the turn of the century. Although the consequences of drug use to their physical health and psychological well-being are not apparent today, the negative effects may become manifest as these users age. Perhaps we should anticipate an increase in rates of disease and a reduction in life expectancy among drug users at a later time. This conjecture, of course, provides no reason to criminalize drug use in the present. We should be extremely reluctant to punish people to protect them from health hazards we *know* to exist. If these risks are merely speculative, the case for punishment evaporates altogether. We might as well speculate that the use of illicit drugs actually improves our health. After all, nearly all researchers now admit that moderate amounts of alcohol correlate with reduced risks of coronary heart disease. We know better than to simply assume without evidence that recreational drug use *must* be very bad for our health in the long run.

The second qualification is more worrisome. Suppose we divide the population of illicit drug users further – into moderate and heavy users. A minority of users have consumed massive amounts of drugs over extended periods of time. Our evidence about the health effects of heavy, long-term illicit drug use – supplemented by data from other countries, where illicit drug use was prevalent at an earlier time than in the United States – does not uniformly show great cause for alarm.[17] Suppose, however, that the latter group turns out to be substantially less healthy than the former. In this event, the controversy would shift to a different issue – a normative issue about criminalization, rather than an empirical issue about the effects of drugs. We have encountered this controversy before, and will do so again. The question is: How would this finding provide a rationale for punishing *all* users of illicit drugs – even those whose drug use does *not* jeopardize their health? After all, moderate users greatly outnumber heavy users. Moreover, heavy users tend to be unlike moderate users; they are far more likely to be poor. What is the justification for punishing everyone who uses an illicit drug in order to protect a minority from becoming less healthy?

The difficulty of answering this question becomes acute when we scrutinize the rationale for punishing users of marijuana – the most popular and least harmful illicit drug. Its health hazards are minimal. In particular, no one has ever been known to die from using marijuana. Thus, the present rationale has virtually no plausibility when applied to this case. Of course, prohibitionists who endorse a health rationale for criminalization will not concede so quickly. We have already examined William Bennett's response: Problem-free users of illicit drugs must be punished so that those who would encounter difficulties are not tempted to begin. Here, the rationale for punishment is somewhat different, but no more persuasive. The case for punishing smokers of marijuana does not focus on the risks of the drug *per se*, but on other risks that are alleged to increase when marijuana is used. In particular, marijuana is often described as the *gateway* drug – the drug that leads users to try other, riskier drugs. I briefly discuss the gateway hypothesis here, but it also plays a central role in other rationales for prohibition, including the two I have already rejected. Prohibitionists who defend the criminalization of marijuana as a means to reduce crime, for example, often admit that smokers are not more likely than non-smokers to commit crimes (when we control for other variables). Still, if marijuana leads to the use of other drugs, which are more plausibly linked to criminality, marijuana might still be prohibited as part of a comprehensive crime-control strategy.

The gateway hypothesis has been widely discredited among researchers; a few statistics suffice to refute it. Admittedly, since marijuana is the most widely used illicit drug, it is often the first illicit drug to be used – although inhalants and psychotherapeutics are more popular among preteens than marijuana. In any event, we should not be surprised to learn that most users of other illicit drugs have tried marijuana first. Most illicit drug users, however, begin with alcohol and tobacco before they smoke marijuana.[18] According to recent surveys, the mean age of first use of marijuana is seventeen, compared with sixteen for alcohol and fifteen for cigarettes. In 1999, 66.7 percent of adolescents who drank heavily were also current users of illicit drugs; only 5.5 percent of non-drinkers were current users of illicit drugs. Prohibitionists often try to support the gateway hypothesis by claiming that adolescents who use marijuana are eighty-five times more likely than abstainers to use cocaine. In reality, however, few users of marijuana graduate to heavy use of other illicit drugs. At least 75 million Americans have tried marijuana. Only one of every 120 of these people currently uses cocaine regularly. Moreover, the rate of progression to other drugs is slowing. Americans born in the 1970s are only half as likely to progress to other drugs as those born in the 1960s.

The claim that punishment is justified to protect the health of illicit drug users gives rise to the same difficulty we have encountered with previous rationales for prohibition. This rationale is plausible only if we are prepared to punish the many in order to protect the few. In the context of the gateway hypothesis, the prohibitionist proposal is as follows. Millions of smokers of marijuana should be punished, because some fraction of them will graduate to more dangerous drugs, and the health of some fraction of these users might deteriorate. Small wonder that our willingness to take such rationales seriously has led to overcriminalization and a massive increase in rates of incarceration in the United States.

Perhaps the central difficulty in assessing the extent to which illicit drugs create risks to health derives from our general misunderstanding of the nature of risk. Obviously, there is *some* level of risk we must be prepared to tolerate before we resort to criminalization. Let us concede, for the sake of argument, that punishment becomes justified beyond this point. How can we begin to identify the level of risk we are willing to accept? Many studies demonstrate that most of us are woefully inept at evaluating risk. Psychologists have described several fallacies to which we typically succumb. We tend, for example, to exaggerate the risk of unfamiliar activities, while minimizing the risk of behaviors to which we are accustomed. We are inclined to overestimate the likelihood of risks that have received lots of publicity. We tend to discount the risk of activities of which we approve. Myriad other examples of our inability to appraise levels of risk could be given.

How, then, can we hope to assess the risks of drug use and decide whether they are beyond an acceptable level? *Aggregate* statistics are helpful in answering this question. According to estimates of the ONDCP, about 25,000 Americans die each year from using illicit drugs. This statistic is not very informative unless it is placed alongside data about the number of fatalities caused by other activities. Here, as elsewhere, aggregate statistics about *licit* drugs provide the most obvious basis of comparison. First, consider the facts about licit drugs used for medical purposes. Approximately 100,000 people die each year from adverse reactions to medications, making prescription drugs one of the leading causes of death in the country. These deaths are due neither to mistakes by doctors who prescribe drugs, nor to patients who take them. Fatal drug reactions occur because virtually all medications have bad side effects in many people, even when taken in proper doses. The assumption that illicit drugs are unsafe, and prescription drugs are safe, is perhaps the greatest myth surrounding the debate about criminalization.

Aggregate statistics about licit drugs used for recreational purposes are an even more obvious basis of comparison. Each year, tobacco kills at least 430,000 people in the United States. The number of annual fatalities caused by alcohol is more controversial, but nearly all estimates exceed 100,000. By contrast, illicit drugs seem benign. Consider the 25,000 casualties said to be caused by illicit drug use. A majority of these deaths are not caused by drugs themselves, but rather by drug prohibition – a point I made in my discussion of drugs and crime, and a point to which I will return in chapter 3. In addition, it is misleading to attribute many of the remaining deaths either to drugs or to drug prohibition. About 2,500 of these fatalities are caused intentionally; 1,460 more are due to injuries inflicted "accidentally or purposely." Illicit drugs themselves cause remarkably few fatalities.

Of course, these aggregate figures do not give us much insight unless they take into account the fact that many more people use licit than illicit drugs. Naturally, we would expect to see more health problems caused by whatever drugs happen to be the most popular. Nonetheless, once we adjust our statistics to reflect this fact – and describe the risk of various drugs as the ratio of fatalities per user – we reach the very same conclusion. When the risk of a given drug is described by the percentage of users who are killed, nicotine is still the most lethal drug by a wide margin. About one-quarter of all persons who smoke a pack of cigarettes daily lose ten to fifteen years of their lives. Illicit drugs are far less hazardous. If criminalization is designed to prevent users from risking their lives, our society has criminalized the wrong drugs.

The point is not simply one of consistency. The question is not: "If the state endeavors to protect public health by punishing people who use cocaine, why doesn't the state also punish people who smoke tobacco and drink alcohol?" After all, problems of consistency can be solved in either of two ways – either by repealing laws against illicit drug use, or by enacting laws against the consumption of alcohol and tobacco. The point is that the latter alternative is unthinkable. Admittedly, several drug policy experts have argued that our regulations governing alcohol are "fantastically permissive."[19] Higher levels of taxation – especially on beer and cigarettes – have been proposed as a way to curb alcohol and tobacco use, particularly among adolescents. But no-one recommends that we should throw smokers and drinkers into jail in order to reduce the health problems caused by licit drugs. Why not? The best answer cites a principle of justice: Punishing smokers or drinkers would be unjust. If we agree with this judgment, the risks of alcohol and tobacco provide an answer to our earlier question. They represent a *baseline* of acceptable risk – a measure of *how much* risk we are willing to tolerate before we resort to the criminal sanction. If illicit drug use creates health risks that are below this baseline, we must conclude that an even greater injustice is perpetrated when users of illicit drugs are punished. The objective, then, is not mere logical consistency. The point is that the criminalization of illicit drugs is unjust for the very same reason as applies to proposals to criminalize the use of licit drugs.

Most prohibitionists are familiar with the foregoing statistics. Still, many of those who try to explain why alcohol and tobacco are exempted from punishment respond that the kinds of fatalities caused by licit drugs are different and less worrisome than those caused by cocaine and heroin. In particular, they point out that illicit drugs can cause *sudden* death – often to users who are young and have many healthy, productive years to live. Even well-conditioned athletes can die instantly from heart attacks caused by heavy cocaine use. Heroin addicts can die quickly from an overdose. By contrast, those who are killed by diseases caused by tobacco or alcohol are more likely to die when they are old. How significant is this claim when assessing this rationale for criminalization?

This claim merits two kinds of replies. First, we should challenge the facts. Although cocaine can cause instant death, the number of such cases is miniscule. We tend to be aware of this risk because of the publicity it receives, not because of the frequency with which it occurs. Heroin overdoses are mysterious; some experts go so far as to denounce them as a myth. Addicts rarely die from pure concentrations of heroin that overwhelm the body. In virtually all cases of alleged heroin overdose, users die from impurities in the drug, or (more commonly) from the toxic effects of other drugs (usually alcohol) that combine with heroin to form a lethal mixture.[20] On other occasions, heroin overdose is caused by the fact that relapsing addicts use doses to which they have lost their tolerance. In any event, we should not pretend that licit drugs like alcohol are incapable of causing sudden death. As many as one-third of the deaths attributed to alcohol are caused by respiratory paralysis produced by an acute dose.[21]

Not only the elderly are affected. College administrators throughout the country are painfully aware of the risk of fatality caused by bing drinking among students.

Apart from these factual challenges, we need to assess the relevance of this claim for our basic question. Why should the fact that some drugs cause death instantly, while other drugs cause death over a longer period of time, be a good reason to punish users of the former drugs, while not criminalizing the use of the latter? This question is especially difficult when the number of deaths caused by licit drugs is so much higher than that caused by illicit drugs – even when the relative risks of each category of drug are expressed as a ratio of fatality per user. The fact that sudden death is caused by activities that do not involve drugs (licit or illicit) is almost never advanced as a reason to criminalize them. Deaths caused by scuba accidents, for example, are usually instantaneous. The occurrence of these deaths does not easily translate into a compelling justification for punishment.

So far, my statistics about the relative risks of licit and illicit drugs involve only fatalities. But the health problems caused by drugs include not only death, but also various diseases and illnesses that lower the quality of life. Allegations about health hazards of illicit drugs are many and varied; it is impossible even to scratch the surface. Drug use has been said to kill brain cells, impair memory and cognition, undermine motivation and performance, produce psychosis and insanity, destroy the immune system, hamper sex drive and reproduction, and generally contribute to hospital emergencies. Obviously, each of these allegations must be assessed drug by drug. How can we begin to get a handle on the health hazards of illicit drugs?

Again, licit drugs provide an obvious basis of comparison. Illicit drugs tend to be less injurious than many licit drugs, recreational or medical. Legal medications cause between 1 million and 5.5 million hospitalizations every year. Approximately 70,000 of these annual hospitalizations are caused by common anti-inflammatories like Advil and Tylenol. But licit drugs used for recreational purposes provide an even more appropriate basis of comparison. Twenty-eight percent of all admissions to one large metropolitan hospital's intensive care units were related to drug problems.

Fourteen percent of these involved tobacco, nine percent involved alcohol, and five percent involved other drugs.[22] Tobacco is a major cause of coronary artery disease, peripheral vascular disease, cerebrovascular diseases, as well as many kinds of cancers. Alcohol is known to be a contributing factor to as many as seventy-five human diseases and conditions, most notably cirrhosis of the liver and cancer of the mouth, throat, esophagus, stomach and liver. Heavy drinkers increase their risk of gastrointestinal disorders, heart disease and high blood pressure. But few known mechanisms plausibly link illicit drug use to common diseases. Admittedly, marijuana smoke is carcinogenic. But for all diseases caused by smoking, the relevant factor is the quantity of smoke inhaled over time. Since users of marijuana smoke so much less than smokers of tobacco products, it is not surprising that epidemiological statistics fail to show higher rates of lung cancer in smokers of marijuana. Cocaine increases the risk of coronary artery disease, which is particularly worrisome for those with pre-existing heart problems – but is not otherwise implicated in common physical diseases. Heavy users may develop paranoia, which includes anxiety, sleeplessness, hypertension, suspicion, and fears of persecution. But many of these same symptoms are common in alcoholics; up to 85 percent of frequent cocaine users are heavy drinkers, making the effects of the two substances difficult to disentangle. Comparable problems surround attempts to measure the health risks of opiates. Heroin addicts tend to lead notoriously unhealthy lifestyles, eating terrible diets, avoiding doctors, and smoking large numbers of cigarettes. But opiates themselves seem to be fairly non-toxic; addicts whose lifestyles are otherwise healthy and who have a steady supply of morphine or heroin suffer primarily from constipation, but have few other difficulties.[23]

Perhaps I miss the most important kind of health problem caused by illicit drug use. Thus far, I have said little about *addiction*. Perhaps drug addiction itself is the disease or illness that prohibition is designed to prevent. According to this school of thought, drug addiction is a medical condition that causes persons to lose control; it makes people virtually powerless to stop using drugs. Enormous debate has surrounded the nature of addiction, and whether it should be categorized as a disease. I offer two simple points in this debate. First, addiction does not begin to distinguish illicit from licit recreational drugs. Depending on how we define and quantify addiction – very controversial matters – tobacco is high (and perhaps first) on the list of addictive drugs. Second, the supposition that addiction is the medical condition that prohibition is designed to prevent is incompatible with well-established doctrines in the criminal law. If addiction were a medical condition, we should be baffled about why it does not constitute an excuse from criminal liability and punishment. I have supposed that people should be punished only when punishment is deserved. But it is hard to argue that people deserve to be punished for having a medical condition that causes them to lose control over whether they will break the law by using drugs. If we really believe that addiction is a medical condition that deprives people of the power to forgo drugs, we surely cannot justify the punishment of addicts. In this book, I am searching for a rationale for criminalization – a reason that justifies our policy of punishing illicit drug users. The supposition that addiction is a medical condition establishes precisely the opposite point. It provides a rationale not to punish, but to create a *defense* from criminal liability and punishment.

Although I have contrasted the health risks of illicit drugs with those of licit drugs, we should look elsewhere – beyond drugs of any kind – to demonstrate the implausibility of using the criminal law to protect people from health risks. Many activities that do not involve the use of a drug are far more risky to health, even though no one would dream of using the criminal law to prohibit them. Melanoma, caused largely by excessive exposure to the sun, kills more people in the United States than all illicit drugs combined. We should rethink our willingness to punish illicit drug users when told that the risks of sun-bathing are greater. But unhealthy foods provide the best source of examples. Every year, according to the Center for Disease Control and Prevention, about 5,000 deaths, 325,000 hospitalizations, and 76 million illnesses are caused by food poisoning. Contamination is only a small part of the problem. More than half of all Americans are now overweight. The 97 million adults who are obese far outnumber illicit drug users, and the health hazards of excessive weight are more easily demonstrated than those of illicit drugs. According to the Center for Disease Control and Prevention, obesity accounts for about

300,000 deaths a year – far more than all illicit and licit drugs (except tobacco) combined. Of course, the number of fatalities does not tell the whole story; obesity diminishes health and the quality of life in myriad ways. For example, the risk of (Type 2) diabetes increases 4 percent for every pound of excess weight. Diabetes is a major cause of blindness, kidney failure and leg amputations, and greatly increases the risk of heart disease and stroke. And diabetes is just one of the many diseases associated with obesity.

High-calorie foods that cause obesity are hardly the only examples that illustrate my point. Illicit recreational drugs do not pose significant health risks relative to any number of recreational activities that we tolerate and even applaud. Mountain climbing is a good illustration. Competitive sports like boxing and rugby provide excellent examples as well. Mothers who would be devastated by the news that their sons are experimenting with drugs are proud to learn that their kids are playing football. But the carnage in the most decrepit crack house is less worrisome than what can be seen on football fields throughout the United States. According to a recent study, 65 percent of professional football players suffer a major injury while playing – that is, an injury that either requires surgery or forces them to miss at least eight games. Two of every three former professionals indicate that their injuries limit their abilities to participate in sports and other recreational activities in retirement. Of course, amateurs are severely injured as well. About one-third of all college football players suffer a concussion; one in five have more than one. Even the most pessimistic estimates of the health risks of illicit drug use are far less shocking.

Of course, the issue of whether a risk should be tolerated depends partly on why people are prepared to take it. Doctors who tested experimental serums on their own bodies are often singled out as heroes, since the potential gains to public health are so great. But competitive sports like rugby are played solely for recreation – for the entertainment of participants and spectators. If we seriously propose using the criminal law against persons who take health risks for frivolous recreational purposes, those who play dangerous sports would have to be punished. This result, of course, would be ludicrous.

In short, no other recreational activity is singled out for severe punishment because of its risks to health. The only conceivable basis for treating illicit drugs differently from other recreational activities is that the former are more risky, by a substantial degree, than the latter. But illicit drug use is *not* more risky than any number of these behaviors. As I have said, illicit drug use is not recommended for persons whose foremost priority is health and safety. But the use of illicit drugs is not especially high on the list of health problems in the United States today.

Perhaps I am mistaken, and illicit drug use creates greater health problems than I have indicated here. Further epidemiological data should help to clarify this issue. But controversies about the exact degree of risk in illicit drug use should not distract us from the issues of principle that (to my mind) are decisive against this purported justification for prohibition. This rationale seems incapable of providing the personal justification for punishment I have sought – a rationale that allows criminalization only when people deserve to be punished for what they have done. Few will assent to the proposition that people deserve to be punished for failing to take proper care of themselves. Nor will they be much more likely to assent to the proposition that people deserve to be punished for engaging in risky behaviors that increase financial burdens for taxpayers. Under this sweeping principle, no baseline of acceptable risk would exist, and all dangerous activities would become subject to criminalization. The many – those whose health is unaffected – would be punished to protect the few.

The health considerations I have discussed in this section might persuade us that we would be foolish to elect to participate in given risky activities. As a matter of public policy, behaviors that pose significant risks to well-being should be discouraged. But these considerations should not convince us to resort to criminalization. We should all welcome state policies to improve health. Punishments, however – especially when they are severe – are simply not an acceptable part of the equation.

DRUGS AND IMMORALITY

Arguably, the foregoing discussions misconstrue the most persuasive kind of justification for drug prohibitions. Perhaps the best rationale for criminalization does not depend on the *effects* or *consequences* of illicit drugs in harming adolescents, causing crime, or contributing to disease and illness. Instead, punishing drug users might represent a *moral* imperative. William Bennett writes: "I find no merit in the legalizers' case. The simple fact is that drug use is wrong. And the moral argument, in the end, is the most compelling argument."[24] Barry McCaffrey, the subsequent drug czar, concurs. President Bush remarks that "legalizing drugs would completely undermine the message that drug use is wrong."[25] James Q. Wilson expresses this view eloquently. He writes:

> Even now, when the dangers of drug use are well-understood, many educated people still discuss the drug problem in almost every way except the right way. They talk about the "costs" of drug use and the "socioeconomic factors" that shape that use. They rarely speak plainly – drug use is wrong because it is immoral and it is immoral because it enslaves the mind and destroys the soul.[26]

As we will see, most people in the United States appear to agree with this moral judgment.

This final rationale for prohibition can be expressed as a *syllogism* – that is, as an argument containing two premises and a conclusion. Although the argument itself admits of several variations, the most straightforward version is as follows. According to the first premise of the argument (the major premise), *the criminal law should punish people who behave immorally*. According to the second premise (the minor premise), *illicit drug use for recreational purposes is immoral*. If these two premises are true, the conclusion of the syllogism is irresistible: The criminal law should punish people for using illicit drugs for recreational purposes. In this section, I will try to show why this syllogism is unsound and fails to provide a persuasive rationale for criminalization. I will argue against both the major and the minor premises of this alleged justification for punishing drug users. I will conclude by suggesting that prohibitionists, rather than those who use drugs, are guilty of the more egregious immorality.

Many legal philosophers would quickly consign this rationale to the category of bad answers I mentioned in chapter 1. That is, many legal philosophers dismiss this rationale out of hand because they reject its major premise – the criminal law should punish people who behave immorally. Philosophers call this premise *legal moralism*. Those who oppose legal moralism do not believe that the criminal law should punish people for immoral behavior. They differ in their reasons for rejecting legal moralism. A few of these theorists claim to be able to make no sense of morality at all, contending it to be a superstition or illusion. No one thinks that we should punish people for reasons that are only superstitions. Most legal philosophers, however, admit that morality makes sense. They agree that the immorality of behavior is relevant to the case for criminalization. After all, the immorality of murder, rape, and theft is central to the justification for punishing these acts. These wrongful activities are criminalized because they harm victims and violate their moral rights. But most legal philosophers insist that immorality is only *necessary*, but not *sufficient* for criminalization. In other words, something in addition to immoral behavior is needed before punishment is justified.

These theorists point out that our system of criminal justice makes no effort to punish *every* instance of immoral behavior – even those that are more clearly immoral than drug use. We do not punish those who lie to their friends, cheat on their exams, or are openly unfaithful to their spouses. I will focus on only one of many possible examples of immorality that is not criminalized – breaches of contract. Suppose that one party deliberately breaks a promise to another that is written in a solemn, binding contract. Parties who break their contractual promises can be sued and ordered to pay monetary damages, but they do not commit crimes for which they can be prosecuted and sent to prison. No one thinks that the law should be changed so that we can begin to punish parties who break their contractual promises. Yet there is little or no dispute that breaking these promises is immoral. Therefore, no one seems to think that *all* immoral conduct should be punished by the criminal law. Apparently, only *some* immoral conduct should be punished. If so, prohibitionists who contend that drug use should be punished because of its immorality should be pressed to provide a reason why *this* case, unlike a case of breaking a contractual promise, should be included among those immoral behaviors the criminal law should punish. Perhaps the rationales I have already examined are attempts to provide such a reason. For example, we might decide to criminalize those cases of immorality that threaten adolescents, increase the risk of crime, or jeopardize our health. But mere immorality, without more, should not be punished. Legal moralism, which allows punishment simply for immorality, should be rejected as a persuasive rationale for criminalization.

Since legal moralism is so unpopular among contemporary legal philosophers, it is not surprising that some prohibitionists avoid explicitly using the word "immoral" in defending this rationale for criminalization. They disguise their endorsement of legal moralism by using language that appears to be morally neutral. For example, a prohibitionist might answer our basic question simply by saying that people should not use drugs. The word "immorality" does not appear in this statement. But how are we to understand the ambiguous word "should"? If the word is used in a *moral* sense – as when someone says that we should not kill or steal – we are back where we began, with the claim that the immorality of drug use is the reason for punishing it.

Of course, the word "should," has many meanings that are *not* moral. On many occasions, the word is used *prudentially* rather than morally – as when we say, for example, that people should not eat so much fat or sugar. Presumably, this statement should be understood to mean that eating too much fat or sugar is unwise or imprudent – not that it is immoral. When "should" is used in this way – to describe what is unwise or imprudent – the claim about drug use is probably correct. We can agree that the use of drugs for recreational purposes *is* often unwise or imprudent. But how does this interpretation of the claim provide a compelling rationale for criminalization? No one seriously believes that the criminal law should punish us for acting unwisely or imprudently – for doing what we shouldn't do, when "should" is construed non-morally. This formulation of the major premise fares even worse than its predecessor – the moral version it was designed to replace. We should be very reluctant to punish immorality, but we should be totally unwilling to punish imprudence or the lack of wisdom. Needless to say, such a principle would subject each of us to punishment on a daily basis.

Yet another version of this rationale for criminalization that seemingly avoids moral language is prevalent in contemporary debates about drug policy. As we have seen, many prohibitionists resist a change in the status quo on the ground that decriminalization would "send the wrong message." This statement is ambiguous and hard to interpret. In all likelihood, it is just another way to express a moral judgment without explicitly using moral terminology. Presumably, the "wrong message" that prohibitionists fear would be "sent" by decriminalization is that drug use is not immoral. If this interpretation captures what prohibitionists have in mind when they complain about the message that decriminialization would send, we have returned to our starting point yet again. What *else* might this statement mean? Other interpretations are possible; perhaps those who worry about the message that is sent by decriminalization are making a prediction about how the incidence of drug use would increase if users were no longer punished. I will address these predictions in chapter 3. At this time, I make a simple point: Any alternative interpretation of this statement is likely to provide a totally unacceptable rationale for criminalization. There is at least some plausibility in supposing that people deserve to be punished when they behave immorally. But there is nothing to be said in favor of the view that people deserve to be punished whenever the failure to do so would "send the wrong message" – when "wrong" is used non-morally.

I conclude that we should reject this first premise in the latest rationale for criminalization – whether or not this premise explicitly contains moral language. In other words, we should reject legal moralism, disguised or otherwise. If I am correct, the entire rationale should be rejected; we need only oppose one premise in a syllogism to oppose the whole argument. If we reject legal moralism, any controversy surrounding the second, minor premise becomes irrelevant. We can concede that recreational drug use is immoral, while denying that this concession provides a rationale for criminalization. But I think we should go further. We must offer a reason to reject this syllogism that should persuade even those few legal philosophers who accept legal moralism – that is, a reason that should convince those who believe that the criminal law *should* punish immorality. To my mind, the second, minor premise in this syllogism is even less plausible than the first. In other words, I see no reason to believe that the recreational use of illicit drugs is immoral. Of course, I may be mistaken in my belief; debates about morality are notoriously hard to resolve. Because *I* see no reason to believe that the recreational use of illicit drugs is immoral does not show that no such reason exists. Before this second premise should be accepted as a good reason to punish drug users, we must evaluate the reasons that lead many people to conclude that recreational drug use is immoral.

What *are* these reasons? How *can* the mere act of taking a substance be immoral? This question raises perhaps the most fascinating and divisive question about contemporary drug policy. Unfortunately, those who are convinced that the recreational use of illicit drugs is immoral almost never try to answer it. That is, they rarely offer a reason in support of their vehement moral condemnation of illicit drug use. Many prohibitionists apparently regard this belief as obvious or self-evident. Clearly, this sort of response – or lack of response – gets us nowhere. As long as beliefs about the immorality of drug use are not defended, we have no way to reply to people who disagree or are undecided, and do not regard these beliefs as obvious or self-evident. Again, our predicament is like that described by David Hume: We are expected to respond to a rationale for criminalization, even though we are kept in the dark about what that rationale is.

Why is the recreational use of illicit drugs thought to be immoral? Demands for a defense of this moral belief are perfectly reasonable. After all, we are not talking about what might be called personal or private morality, as when we say that I have my morality, and you have yours. We are talking about the kind of morality that provides a basis for punishing others – even those who do not share the same moral beliefs as the people who punish them. When morality is cited as a basis for criminalization, legal moralists typically have no difficulty in defending their beliefs about the immorality of the acts they punish. Murder, rape, and robbery are immoral because they violate rights and severely harm victims. All persons have moral rights to life, personal security, and property; harmful acts that violate these rights are clearly immoral. But this defense, we should recall, is not available to prohibitionists who allege that recreational drug use is immoral. Recreational drug users – like those described in my anecdotes in chapter 1 – need not harm or violate the rights of anyone. If recreational drug use is indeed immoral, we need a different reason for this belief than is available in the case of these familiar and uncontroversial crimes.

Sometimes, prohibitionists appeal to public opinion polls to try to support their belief that the recreational use of illicit drugs is immoral. They point to surveys that indicate that roughly two-thirds of Americans agree that illicit drug use is morally wrong. Sixty-four percent say that marijuana use is morally wrong. Seventy-six percent report they would continue to oppose the legalization of cocaine and heroin, even if they could be guaranteed that it would lead to less crime. This latter statistic suggests that public resistance to decriminalization may derive more from morality than from any of the rationales I have examined in the previous sections of this chapter.[27]

For at least three reasons, however, these public opinion polls fail to show that the recreational use of illicit drugs is immoral and should be punished. The first point is the most obvious: moral controversies are simply not resolved by surveys of this kind. Consider, for example, vegetarians who insist that eating animals is immoral. Perhaps these vegetarians have good reasons in favor of their beliefs, or perhaps they do not. But we do not prove them to be mistaken by reminding them that a majority of the public in both the United States and England disagree with their position. Unquestionably, vegetarians *know* that the majority rejects their beliefs; they are prepared to argue that most people are mistaken about the morality of eating meat. We could make no sense of the claim that the majority might be mistaken about morality if disputes of this kind could be resolved by a poll.

Next, we should not be surprised to learn that the answers respondents give to pollsters are greatly affected by exactly how the question is phrased. When people are asked whether they believe that drug use is immoral, they may think that they are being asked about what I have called personal or private morality – about what they believe is immoral for them. Respondents are less likely to judge that *others* behave immorally when they use drugs. They are even less likely to say that other people deserve to be punished for their immoral use of drugs. Only 51 percent say both that the use of marijuana is morally wrong and should not be tolerated. Public support erodes still further when respondents are asked whether others deserve to be punished *severely* for their immoral use of drugs.

Finally and most controversially, I think we are entitled to draw exactly the opposite conclusion from these surveys. We had better have a very powerful consensus about the immorality of given kinds of behavior before we should feel confident about punishing those who disagree with us. Legal moralists are not hesitant to punish murderers, rapists and robbers, since no one defends the moral permissibility of these acts. But 49 percent of American respondents do *not* agree with the statement that all illicit drug use is morally wrong and intolerable. About 14 percent of Americans believe that all drugs should be legalized. A recent ABC News poll found that 69 percent of adults in the United States say they would favor state laws that require treatment instead of incarceration for first and second non-violent drug offenses. No other crime – at least no other crime for which punishments are severe – gives rise to such disagreement and ambivalence in the public. When such significant numbers dissent, we should be willing to entertain the possibility that the majority might be mistaken and the minority might be correct. Prohibitionists who defend criminalization on the ground that polls reveal drug use to be immoral should be embarrassed rather than vindicated when the data reveal the extent to which our citizenry is so deeply divided.

So our question remains: Why should we believe that the recreational use of illicit drugs is immoral? Sometimes, prohibitionists offer historical explanations. They remind Americans of our puritan legacy, of our long-standing suspicion of pleasure and fun, of our alleged "hedonism taboo." But how are these points supposed to advance our inquiry? They cannot be taken seriously as a *justification* for criminalization. Whatever may have been true at an earlier period in our history, no one continues to believe that an activity is immoral simply because it produces pleasure. No one denounces other activities as wrongful – spectator sports and television, for example – on the grounds that they are recreational. As I will argue in chapter 3, the value of recreation provides a better basis to defend than to condemn the morality of illicit drug use.

How *might* a moral case against recreational drug use be constructed? Someone could believe this activity to be wrongful for either of two kinds of reasons. First, drugs might be thought to be immoral because of the psychological states they cause. In other words, the "high" of drugs might be wrongful for people to experience. This alternative seems improbable. In the first place, it is not altogether clear how a psychological state *could* be immoral to experience. Moreover, the euphoria produced by licit drugs and prescription medications are almost never condemned as wrongful. In addition, psychological states that may be indistinguishable from those caused by drugs – a "runner's high," for example – are not denounced. Therefore, the moral case against drugs cannot be based on the nature of the experiences they cause. More likely, the alleged immorality consists in the behavior of persons under the influence of drugs. Specifically, drugs produce risks that users will behave badly. But this case against drugs flounders in light of the empirical considerations I have already discussed. Few drug users jeopardize the welfare of children, commit crimes, endanger their health to a substantial degree, or otherwise behave in ways that merit blame or condemnation. Since neither of these two explanations of the immorality of drug use seem plausible, it is hard to see how a persuasive case *could* be constructed.

No defense has yet been provided for the minor premise in our syllogism. In other words, we have found no reason to believe that the recreational use of (some) drugs is immoral. Where, then, do we stand with respect to this fourth and final rationale for selective prohibition? Before proceeding, let me clarify my position in two respects. First, I am not saying that no sensible moral objections have ever been raised against recreational drug use. Instead, I am saying that the *kinds* of moral objections that are plausible provide a poor rationale for criminalization. Let me explain. In my judgment, the most serious moral questions about recreational drug use invoke a conception of human virtue. Philosophers have long disagreed about the details of a theory of human excellence. Greek philosophers and Christian theologians, for example, have offered very different accounts of perfection in human beings. All philosophers, however, agree that the ideal person cultivates his physical and intellectual talents. Drug use, especially when excessive, undermines this aspiration;

these users tend to make less of their lives than they might. Heavy drug use might be described as a *handicap*.[28] Those who use drugs excessively for an extended period of time are destined to fall short of an ideal. According to this school of thought, heavy drug use is a moral *vice* – the opposite of a virtue.

Whether *all* recreational drug use is a vice is far more controversial. Philosophers who develop accounts of human excellence disagree about the extent to which the pursuit of pleasure is consistent with the attainment of virtue. Notwithstanding ascetic accounts of virtue, which condemn all pleasurable activities, I see no reason to believe that those who aspire to perfection cannot pursue recreational activities at least occasionally. Perhaps recreational *drug* use, unlike other recreational pursuits, is incompatible with virtue. But this claim needs to be defended rather than assumed.

In any event, the difficulty with this kind of moral position should be evident. No one seriously proposes to criminalize all vice. It is one thing to say that we deserve to be punished when we behave immorally, but quite another to say that we deserve to be punished when we handicap ourselves or fall short of an ideal. Sloth and gluttony are at odds with the development of our physical and intellectual talents, but almost all of us would be subject to punishment if these vices were criminalized. A rationale for criminalization must show that drug use is wrongful – not that it is contrary to virtue or excellence. The criminal law establishes a floor beneath which we are not permitted to sink, rather than a ceiling to which we are encouraged to aspire.

A second clarification is needed. I am not insisting that no good reason *can* be given for concluding that the recreational use of illicit drugs is immoral. Again, a negative is notoriously hard to prove. I am only saying that no good reason *has* been given in support of this moral conclusion. Here, as elsewhere, the case for criminalization has not been made. I invite and encourage those prohibitionists who believe that illicit drug use is immoral to rise to the challenge and provide a good reason why we should share their belief. Until such a reason is given, even confirmed legal moralists should be unwilling to punish recreational users of illicit drugs.

Are there any reasons to believe that the recreational use of illicit drugs is *not* immoral? I think so. After all, almost no one believes that the recreational use of *all* drugs is immoral. Recall that prohibition is selective. Few of us believe that people behave immorally when they use alcohol, caffeine, or tobacco products. Moral condemnation is generally reserved for those drugs that are illicit. Is there a relevant difference between those drugs that morality permits and those that morality (allegedly) prohibits? If not, we have good reason to suspect that moral objections to illicit drugs are an unfounded prejudice. We must ask: From a moral point of view, is there good reason to distinguish between the use of licit and illicit drugs?

I suspect that most attempts to answer this question will rehearse one of the other rationales for criminalization I have already critiqued. In other words, those who believe that the recreational use of *illicit* drugs is immoral, but condone the recreational use of *licit* drugs, generally try to distinguish between the two kinds of substances by claiming that the former are especially dangerous for children, linked to crime, or risky to health. If this answer is given, we do not really have a new rationale for criminalization – a rationale that is different from those discussed above. The rationale appears to be new because it is couched in moral language. In fact, however, it simply uses moral language to express one of the rationales for criminalization we have previously examined and found to be deficient.

But a moral defense of selective prohibition need not rehearse one of the foregoing rationales for criminalization. Sometimes moral condemnation is reserved for illicit drugs because they are said to be implicated in a more amorphous sense that society is deteriorating. According to this school of thought, the recreational use of illicit drugs is not wrongful because it directly causes some particular problem, but because it is indirectly responsible for a wide variety of social ills. Illicit drug use has been blamed for break-ups in marriage, trends in teenage pregnancies, the erosion of civil discourse, a worsening of education, a decline in religious faith, and just about everything else that is said to be wrong with contemporary society. Real evidence linking drug use to these social pathologies is rarely produced. Moreover, alcohol is more strongly implicated in most of these effects. Demographics help to explain the perception that illicit drugs in particular contribute to social decay. Our attitudes about given drugs are shaped by our attitudes about the persons who use them. Illicit drug use is prevalent among adolescents and young adults. Most quit using illicit drugs before they reach middle-age. Licit drugs, by contrast, are more likely to be used throughout entire lifetimes. Every generation of adults has accused the next generation of leading society downhill. The fact that illicit drugs tend to be used most widely by the very group of persons who are always blamed for social deterioration does not express a real relationship of cause and effect.

A few prohibitionists have risen to the challenge and endeavored to explain why they believe that the recreational use of illicit drugs is immoral, whereas the recreational use of licit drugs is not. James Q. Wilson writes:

> If we believe – as I do – that dependency on certain mind-altering drugs is a moral issue, and that their illegality rests in part on their immorality, then legalizing them undercuts, if it does not eliminate altogether, the moral message. That message is at the root of the distinction we now make between nicotine and cocaine. Both are highly addictive; both have harmful physical effects. But we treat the two drugs differently, not simply because nicotine is so widely used to be beyond the reach of effective prohibition, but because its use does not destroy the user's essential humanity. Tobacco shortens one's life, cocaine debases it. Nicotine alters one's habits, cocaine alters one's soul.[29]

How are we to understand this attempt to differentiate between the morality of licit and illicit drug use? After all, Wilson does not mention the protection of youth, a rise in crime, a decline in health, or a general deterioration in society to support the distinction he draws. Wilson's reference to the "soul" provides the key to an answer. The use of illicit drugs is said to "alter" or "destroy" the soul. On the basis of this allegation, Wilson is prepared to send illicit drug users to prison, while sparing those who use licit drugs like tobacco and alcohol. How might his allegation be assessed? Millions of living Americans have used cocaine and heroin. If we examine their souls, would we find them to be altered or destroyed? Would we find the souls of users of licit drugs to be preserved and intact?

I cannot really believe that Wilson is intending to make an empirical claim about what doctors and scientists would discover if they examined the souls of illicit drug users. Instead, I believe he is using religious grounds to object to the use of illicit drugs. Contemporary discussions of drug policy rarely mention religion explicitly. I believe this neglect is unfortunate; religion plays an absolutely central role in shaping contemporary drug policy. In chapter 1, I encouraged readers to begin the debate about drug policy by asking friends and neighbors whether they really believe that people should be punished simply for using illicit drugs. Unfortunately, I cannot guarantee that even those friends and neighbors who generally welcome intellectual exchange will be eager to entertain this question. Frank discussions of drug policy are likely to provoke hostility and anger. Few people seem willing to examine this issue dispassionately. Fair-minded citizens are generally prepared to consider and evaluate competing arguments about the merits or demerits of policies involving such issues as education, health care, and social security. Drug policy, by contrast, tends to evoke a very different kind of response. Although reasonable arguments can be made on both sides, a discussion of this issue will not always be civil or friendly.

Why do controversies about drugs tend to cause people to become so angry and emotional? No single answer accounts for the passion people seem to feel about this issue. To a large extent, however, the inability or unwillingness to engage in a civil and informed debate about illicit drugs reflects the fact that personal opinion on this issue tends to be strongly influenced by religion. Attitudes about drugs and drug policy correlate with age, race, geographical location, political affiliation, and gender. But no demographic variable correlates nearly as strongly with attitudes about illicit drugs as religion. Lifetime abstainers frequently mention religion when asked to explain how they have managed to resist the lure of illicit drugs. Polls in 1999 indicate that a majority of respondents who identify themselves as having "no religion" believe that marijuana should be "made legal." Protestants, by contrast, oppose legalization by a 69-26 margin. The United States is probably more religious than any Western industrialized democracy; it is no coincidence that the United States has the most punitive drug policy. We should not be surprised that issues closely linked to religion are impossible to resolve by rational argument. In this respect, attitudes about drugs resemble those about abortion, where religion plays an even more central role. Religious belief is, almost by definition, the product of faith rather than reason.

Of course, religious belief provides a bad reason to punish drug users. Our basic question asks for a reason that justifies the punishment of drug users. Religious belief provides no real answer to this question because it fails to offer *a reason* at all. We live in a secular state in which people should not be punished for behaving in ways that are contrary to the teachings of religion. A justification for punishment must not presuppose that we all share the same religious faith.

Nothing more needs to be said to show why religious belief provides a bad answer to our basic question. But I think it is important to go further. One of the frustrating aspects of debating an issue that is influenced by religion is that those who take sides are not always candid about why they hold their opinions. Few are willing to say, "I believe that drug users should be punished because of my religious convictions." Instead, they often disguise the reasons for their beliefs. For example, almost everyone who thinks that the earth is only 6,000 years old, or that human beings did not evolve from some other species, holds these beliefs on religious grounds. But many of these people defend their positions not by mentioning religion, but by poking holes in the arguments of geologists or evolutionary biologists. Those who are convinced of the truth of evolution can always respond in kind. But evidence about the fossil record is quite beside the point in addressing why these people actually hold their beliefs. Debates will have no impact as long as we focus on issues that do not really explain why parties to the debate feel as they do.

Although I am well aware of the remarkable correlation between respondents who strongly favor punishing drug users and those who identify themselves as deeply religious, the connection between religious faith and drug prohibition is not especially clear. People who draw inspiration from religious texts like the Bible can (and do) quote scripture in support of their positions about many criminal laws. They have no difficulty locating prohibitions against theft and murder in the Bible. They can find textual support for their position on abortion. But the Bible says virtually nothing about drugs. Some religions (such as Rastafarians) actually quote the Bible *in support* of their illicit drug use. The drug issue illustrates the well-known fact that religious texts are subject to very different interpretations. Religious opposition to illicit drugs, like non-religious moral opposition, is a conclusion in search of a reason to support it.

I conclude that we should reject both the major and the minor premises in this syllogism for criminalization. We should be unwilling to allow people to be punished simply because their behavior is immoral. Even more importantly, we have no good reason to believe that the recreational use of illicit drugs *is* immoral. Therefore, this rationale for criminalization fares no better than its predecessors. But one more crucial point remains to be made before we leave this rationale behind. Prohibitionists pretend to occupy the moral high ground in debates about illicit drug use. Unlike their opponents, they profess to stand up against immorality. Those who oppose criminalization are seemingly placed in the uncomfortable and awkward position of condoning behavior that is suspect from a moral point of view.

The moral high ground should *not* be conceded to those who favor prohibition. Disagreement about the immorality of recreational drug use is reasonable. But there can be no disagreement about the immorality of punishing people without excellent reasons to do so. Punishment is the most powerful weapon available to the state, and we must always be vigilant to ensure that it is not inflicted without adequate justification. The entire thrust of this book is that this weapon is invoked without good reason against recreational drug users. If I am correct, prohibitionists are more clearly guilty of immorality than their opponents. The wrongfulness of recreational drug use, if it exists at all, pales against the immorality of punishing drug users. In chapter 1, I related anecdotes to describe the immorality of criminalization in personal terms. In chapter 3, I will argue that the immorality of prohibition affects us all, users and non-users alike. How much harm to drug users and to society are prohibitionists willing to tolerate in their efforts to prevent people from using drugs? I conclude that those who punish drug users perpetrate a far greater immorality than those who use drugs.

In this chapter, I have tried to show that no good reason has been given to punish people simply for using (some) drugs for recreational purposes. No persuasive answer to our basic question has been given. The reasons I have surveyed are not good enough – not nearly good enough – to justify prohibition.

As I have indicated, however, my case against prohibition might be unsound. Perhaps one of the reasons I have addressed is better than I believe it to be. Perhaps some reason I have not examined can be defended. Perhaps several bad reasons can be combined into a persuasive case over-all. Prohibitionists should be required to select one of these options. They should be forced to defend prohibition – a challenge they have avoided. Otherwise, we are entitled to conclude that criminal laws that punish people for using recreational drugs are unjust and should be changed.

Every reasonable person is concerned about the welfare of adolescents, worried about crime, anxious to improve public health, and opposed to immorality. Despite these concerns, I have argued that punishing illicit drug users is unjust. The general difficulty with thinking that punishment is justified in order to protect children, reduce crime, improve health or prevent immorality is that these strategies are *overinclusive*. In other words, each of these alleged justifications for punishing illicit drug users suffers from a common defect: They sweep far too broadly. They allow a great many persons to be punished in order to prevent a harm that will be caused by only a small minority. Only a tiny percentage of the 80 or 90 million illicit drug users have ever gone on to harm themselves or anyone else. We should oppose a strategy of casting the net of criminality so widely. An adequate rationale for punishment must be personal. It must provide a justification for punishing each and every drug user, not only those who cause the various harms I have described here. We should not turn vast numbers of people into criminals in order to prevent the mis-deeds of a few.

My arguments do not prove too much. They do not undermine the justifiability of criminal laws we know to be defensible. Criminal laws are obviously needed to prohibit acts that intentionally and directly victimize other human beings. No one seriously questions the legitimacy of criminal laws against acts that harm innocent victims. There is no movement to decriminalize assault or battery. As we move beyond offenses that violate rights, criminalization becomes more difficult to defend. Prohibitionists have failed to do the hard work of justifying their decision to punish recreational users of illicit drugs.

3

DISADVANTAGES OF PROHIBITION

POSITIVE EFFECTS OF DRUGS

The argument against criminalization presented in chapter 2 does not presuppose that recreational drug use has any positive benefits. My position thus far is that the reasons in favor of selective prohibition are not good enough to justify the drastic step of punishing drug users. This position is consistent with the belief that recreational drug use has no value whatever – no more value than pointless acts like digging a hole and filling it up. So far, the argument is incomplete. Suppose I am correct that we lack a good reason to punish drug users. We might still ask: How good a reason do we really need? Since punishment is the worst thing our state can do to us, I have suggested that the justification for punishing anyone – drug users, or those who dig holes and fill them up – had better be strong.

But the strength of the reason we require cannot be unrelated to the value of the activity for which punishment is imposed. Is it equally unjust to punish drug users and, say, readers of books? In the latter case, I assume that we lack good reasons to punish. Similarly, I have argued that we lack good reasons to punish drug users. But I also believe that punishing readers of books would be a greater injustice than punishing drug users. The difference between these two cases seems clear. Punishing readers of books would be unjust not only because we *lack* good reasons *to* punish, but also because we *have* good reasons *not* to punish. Can the same be said of those who use illicit drugs for recreational purposes? If drug use has absolutely no value, we should demand less of a reason before we allow it to be criminalized. But if drug use has value, we should demand a better reason to criminalize it. Moreover, we are more likely to decide that illicit drug use is morally acceptable if we believe it to produce a result we can describe as good or beneficial. Therefore, a full evaluation of the injustice of punishing drug users depends on whether we attach any value to the use of drugs for recreational purposes. Is there some good that is brought about by recreational drug use? In other words, does recreational drug use have any positive value? In this section, I will attempt to answer this important question. Ultimately, I will try to describe what I take the value of recreational drug use to be. First, however, I want to indicate why the question itself is peculiar and difficult to answer.

Since at least the time of Plato, moral and political philosophers have differed in their attempts to describe the nature of a just society. According to a prominent school of thought, one society is more just than another to the extent that its political institutions promote objective values. The task of the philosopher is to identify valuable activities; the job of the politician is to design institutions that enable citizens to engage in them. But a second school of thought differs radically about the nature of a just society. Philosophers should not try to provide an exhaustive list of valuable activities. Instead, they should acknowledge *pluralism:* citizens have very different views about which activities are valuable, and no philosophical argument can show that only one such view is correct. According to this conception, politicians should design institutions that allow citizens the freedom to pursue whatever activities they have decided to be valuable.

If we tend to favor the second conception of a just society, we must be prepared to recognize that many people will elect to engage in activities that seem strange and unusual to many of us. In exercising their freedom of choice, individuals often come to care passionately about pursuits that appear to be trivial or meaningless to others. Any number of examples could be given; I will mention only one. Most of us are acquainted with fanatical football fans. They follow their favorite team around the country. Every victory fills them with pride and glee; every loss is an occasion for gloom and despair. Notice how difficult it would be for a fan to defend his passion if he were called upon to do so. After all, none of his friends or relatives is a member of his team; he does not know any players personally.

He would probably admit that he would feel just as passionately about a different team if he had been born in some other city. He has no financial stake in the prosperity of his team. Yet there is not much in life he cares about more deeply than the success of his favorite team.

Fortunately, our fanatical fan need *not* defend his passion. The state does not tell him that his preferred activity lacks value and is unimportant. A philosopher who reported that he could find no value in this activity would be told by the fan to mind his own business. We do not demand that those who enjoy such pursuits must explain exactly why they attach so much meaning to them. We allow people the liberty to act according to their own preferences, however odd they may seem to the rest of us. This willingness is the central mark of a free society. Of course, I do not mean to suggest that we have an unlimited freedom to find value in *any* activity. Surely it *is* the business of the state when someone claims to find value in murder or mayhem. These crimes are concerns of the state because a just society protects the rights of persons who are victimized by these harmful activities. The football fan, however, need not harm or violate the rights of anyone.

The difficulty of defending the value of an activity is especially acute when it is purely recreational – pursued for pleasure, euphoria, satisfaction, or some other positive psychological state. If I find a given activity to be enjoyable, I am often at a loss to explain my reaction to someone who disagrees with me. This is certainly true of taste in foods. Suppose that I love the flavor of broccoli or anchovies. How can I possibly hope to persuade someone who detests these foods to share my preferences? Clearly, the whole endeavor is strange. Why should we have to defend the value of the fun and enjoyment we experience when we engage in an activity we like? We should not be made to feel shallow and superficial when we admit that our only reason for doing something is because we find it to be pleasant and enjoyable. Much of what we care about is purely recreational. Many moral philosophers have claimed that pleasure is intrinsically valuable. In fact, some have gone so far as to say that pleasure (and the absence of pain) is the *only* thing that is intrinsically valuable.

Nor should we be apologetic or embarrassed if the particular activity we find to be pleasant and enjoyable involves the use of a *drug*. Invariably, the decision to use illicit drugs for recreational purposes is attributed to peer pressure, boredom, alienation, immaturity, ignorance, depression, or some other pathology. Empirical support for these preconceptions is dubious; a recent survey of 15,000 adolescents conducted by the Schools Health Education Unit in Exeter, England, found that young people with high self-esteem were more likely to use licit drugs than those whose self-confidence was low. In any event, no one proposes comparable pathological explanations about the popularity of *licit* drugs. Punishment or mandatory treatment is never recommended for wine connoisseurs. Like much else about prohibition, attitudes about *why* people use drugs are extraordinarily selective. But people have exactly the same reasons to use licit and illicit drugs. After all, no known societies – except perhaps that of Eskimos – refrain from using drugs for recreational purposes. Drug use is so pervasive that researchers like Andrew Weil have speculated that "the desire to alter consciousness periodically is an innate, normal drive analogous to hunger or the sexual drive."[30]

Why is the recreational value of illicit drugs so difficult to comprehend and acknowledge? We should recognize a widespread psychological tendency to *de*value activities that we ourselves do not like. Those who love to climb mountains can appreciate the exhilaration of another climber. But those who do not share this passion may be at a loss to fathom why anyone would bother to make the effort. This psychological tendency is pervasive in our attitudes about drugs – both licit and illicit. If we dislike the smell of cigars, we cannot understand how anyone could possibly enjoy them. In our more thoughtful moments, however, we realize that tastes differ, and that our own preferences give us no reason to limit the freedom of those who disagree with us.

With these observations in mind, consider the remark of William Bennett about the preferences of illicit drug users. According to Bennett, "a citizen in a drug-induced haze ... is not what the founding fathers meant by the 'pursuit of happiness.'"[31] It is tempting to respond to Bennett's claim by setting the historical record straight. Drug use – much of it illicit – was hardly unknown among the founding fathers. But the more basic point is not historical. Bennett distorts and misrepresents the wisdom of those who created the political system in which we live. In a free society, the state is no more entitled to devalue the activity of the drug user than that of the fanatical football fan.

To this point, I have called attention to the peculiarity of demanding that the recreational user of illicit drugs defend his preference. We do not impose comparable requirements on those who watch soap operas or patronize amusement parks. But we cannot expect to satisfy those who make this demand by telling them to mind their own business. In fact, the value of drug use *can* be defended. Many opponents of prohibition have gone to great lengths to describe the values of drug use in terms that others can understand. The most familiar strategy is to show how the use of drugs may help to promote some objective that is universally acknowledged to be valuable. Some have contended that drug use has spiritual benefits. Early researchers of LSD insisted that it opened doors of enlightenment. Others have emphasized the advantages of drugs in fostering literary and artistic creativity. Opium helped Coleridge to produce remarkable poetry. Of course, prohibitionists scoff at these statements. In what follows, however, I will not explore these benefits in any detail; I make no grandiose claims about the value of illicit drugs. My focus is on *recreational* drug use. The above advantages of illicit drugs fall outside the vague boundary of recreational use.

Still, I intend to pursue a similar strategy. That is, I believe the value of recreational drug use is best described by showing how it helps to achieve an objective that everyone recognizes to be important. In chapter 1, I questioned a cornerstone of our drug policy – the distinction between recreational and medical drug use. When a contrast proves very difficult to draw, we must be sure that we have a good reason to make the effort. The reason for trying to salvage the distinction between recreation and medicine, I believe, is that the value of health is beyond controversy. We allow people to take enormous risks in pursuing an objective we admit to be important. We sympathize and understand when individuals use drugs to treat a medical condition – a condition that qualifies as a disease or illness. Recreation, on the other hand, is regarded as much less important. The dangers of a drug are not worth risking when that drug is used simply to gain pleasure or euphoria.

To illustrate these claims, consider the controversy surrounding prozac, the popular antidepressant. Perhaps 40 million people have used this drug since its introduction in 1988. Most users believe prozac to be helpful in treating a variety of psychiatric disorders. Of course, the long-term effects of prozac are unknown. Most everyone admits that it has undesirable side effects, such as the loss of sex drive. In addition, those who stop taking prozac frequently experience flu-like withdrawal symptoms. Other allegations are far more worrisome. One doctor estimates that prozac has led 25,000 people to commit suicide who would not have done so otherwise. No one can be sure whether this estimate is accurate. My point is that the state would never tolerate the recreational use of a drug if reputable doctors alleged its side effects to be so severe. Recreational users who were willing to take these risks would be sent directly to jail. But we allow users to run these risks without fear of punishment because we classify the condition treated by prozac as a disease or illness.

Of course, no drug is without risks and side effects. According to some recent estimates, prescription drugs cause about 100,000 fatalities each year in the United States – even when these drugs are taken exactly as prescribed. This figure far exceeds the most pessimistic estimates of deaths caused by illicit drugs.[32] Why do we tolerate these enormous risks? The answer can only be the value we attach to health. When drugs used for recreational purposes give rise to relatively minor risks – as with allegations that the dehydration associated with ecstasy has caused a few fatalities – the state responds by increasing the severity of criminal penalties. Why do we not allow these lesser risks? Again, the answer can only be the lack of value we attach to recreation. The key to understanding our present drug policy, then, is to realize that recreational drug taking is regarded as having so little value that it fails to justify even the smallest risks. This is why our drug policy places medical and recreational use in entirely different categories.

We encounter these attitudes again and again. An advisory committee of the FDA recently voted to approve Uprima (although the manufacturer subsequently withdrew the marketing application). The committee recommended that Uprima be made available by prescription, despite findings that one in thirty men who were given the optimal dose fainted or suffered seriously low blood pressure. In one test, a man under the influence of Uprima crashed his car into a fence. "There will be some people who will probably lose their lives because they pass out at the top of the stairs or are operating a car" when they faint, warned an FDA adviser and cardiologist. "This drug is clearly going to kill some people," agreed another.[33] Still, both doctors joined the majority of nine to three in voting to approve the drug, which received its European license in 2001 and is now available in England. Apparently, several deaths are a price worth paying for the benefits of treating erection dysfunction – a condition we classify as a syndrome or illness. Only our willingness to categorize the use of Uprima as medical would lead us to accept risks of this magnitude.

Our refusal to tolerate any level of risk when drug use is recreational is very hard to defend. Notice that we allow people to take enormous risks when they engage in recreational activities that do *not* involve the use of drugs. Consider the risks of sky-diving, skiing, or scuba diving. These recreational activities are dangerous – more dangerous than any widely used illicit drug. Still, we do not require individuals to have a very good reason, such as a disease or illness, before we allow these risks to be taken. Why not? The answer is that we attach value to these activities. More precisely, we are willing to allow people to decide for themselves whether they value these activities. Even when we do not fathom why anyone would jump out of an airplane with a parachute simply for the thrill, we defer to the judgments of those who disagree with us about whether such activities are valuable and worth the danger. Sometimes we even admire people who undertake enormous risks in recreational activities like mountain climbing. Why, then, are medical reasons required before we allow people to undertake the (lesser) risks inherent in drugs? Why do we punish people for the risks they take by using illicit drugs recreationally, when virtually no other dangerous recreational activity is punished? I have no good answers to these important questions, which lie at the foundation of our drug policy.

Recreation is valuable. We all know this to be true, despite the curious and indefensible exception that is made when illicit drugs provide the source of the positive psychological state we seek when engaging in a recreational activity. To inquire more deeply into the nature of this value, we need to be more precise about why so many people use drugs – licit or illicit – for recreational purposes. Surprisingly little research on this topic exists. Of course, no single explanation can be given. The best explanation, however, is *mood control*. We often say that moods are beyond our control and "come over us," but these statements are exaggerations. In fact, we have many devices to help us to alter our moods. Drugs play a central role in this process. The particular circumstances in which different licit drugs are used provide the key to their appeal. Caffeine is used mostly in the morning, when people are drowsy and lethargic. Alcohol is used mostly in the evening, when people want to unwind and relax. Without recreational drugs, many would be condemned to remain sleepy in the morning, and tense in the evening. These drugs allow us to change our moods in desired ways at given times and places. By this means, users of licit drugs exercise more control over their lives and thereby increase their enjoyment.

This explanation is equally applicable to illicit drugs. Users take them in order to alter their mood in desired directions. The oldest literary accounts of illicit drugs illustrate this phenomenon. In the *Odyssey*, Homer describes the use of nepenthe, an opium preparation. When Telemachus visited Sparta, the memory of soldiers killed in the Trojan War was so distressing that "Helen, daughter of Zeus, poured a drug, nepenthe, into the wine they were drinking which made them forget all evil. Those who drank of the mixture did not shed a tear all day long, even if their mother or father had died, even if a brother or beloved son was killed before their own eyes." Today, interviews with recreational users of illicit drugs consistently indicate that people choose which drugs to take, and when to take them, in order to feel the way they believe is appropriate for the situation. Marijuana is used to "relax;" LSD is taken to "have fun;" amphetamines and ecstasy are taken to become "energetic."[34] Of course, users do not always *succeed* in achieving the mood they desire. But no recreational activity is uniformly rewarding.

My argument in chapter 2 was designed to show that we do not have good reasons to punish recreational users of illicit drugs. These arguments do not presuppose that recreational drug use has any positive value. In this section, I have argued that we have good reasons *not* to punish recreational users of illicit drugs. This argument *does* suppose that recreational drug use has positive value, and I have tried to describe the nature of this value. I have tried not to exaggerate the extent of this value. I have not relied on grand claims that portray drugs as the key to spiritual enlightenment. Most of the value of recreational drug use consists in simple fun and euphoria – goods that should require no elaborate defense. More specifically, the ability to alter mood in desired ways at given times and places can increase control over life and add to its enjoyment. Our assessment of the injustice of prohibition is incomplete unless we take the value of illicit drug use into account. When this value is added to the inquiry, the injustice of punishing recreational users of illicit drugs becomes even more apparent.

Negative effects of prohibition

So far, I have argued that the state lacks a good reason to punish illicit drug users, and has a good reason not to punish illicit drug users. In combination, these arguments show prohibition to be unjust. The injustice of criminalization provides the best reason to abandon punitive policies that fill our jails and prisons with illicit drug users. But some readers may still be unmoved – even if they accept my arguments to this point. The considerations I have described may seem too abstract and distant from our personal experience to change our minds. If our own friends or families are unlikely to face punishment, we may not care about the injustice done to others. After all, the drugs that most of *us* use are not prohibited. Surely criminalization has achieved some benefits, even though the rationales in its favor are less persuasive than we would like. And what harm does prohibition really bring about? Of course, it harms the victims of injustice, but how does that affect the rest of us? Unfortunately, the world is full of injustice. Why should we be concerned about *this* injustice in particular?

In this section, I will try to answer this question. Although justice provides the *best* reason to oppose prohibition, it does not provide the *only* reason. Drug prohibition has caused a great deal of harm – harm that affects us all, whether or not we ever face punishment for using an illicit drug. Our drug policy harms us all because it is *counterproductive*. In this section, I will describe several bad consequences that are caused by our insistence that illicit drug users be punished. Criminalization would have to accomplish enormous benefits in order to justify a policy that produces all of the harms I will describe. I believe that our punitive policies do *not* accomplish nearly enough benefits to outweigh these harms. On this ground alone, decriminalization represents a preferable drug policy. Therefore, we have additional reasons to reject prohibition. Even if injustice does not move us to oppose criminalization, more can be said against our policy than that it treats drug users unjustly.

In this section I list eight respects in which our policy of punishing illicit drug users is counterproductive. In other words, I describe eight distinct bad consequences of prohibition. I do not pretend that this list is exhaustive; criminalization is undoubtedly counterproductive in many ways I do not mention. The discussions that follow are cursory and incomplete; books could be written about each of these harmful consequences of prohibition. In most cases, books *have* been written. Since other critics of criminalization have examined these problems in greater detail, and because my own focus is on the injustice of prohibition, my discussion of the following problems is brief.

1. Racial Bias

Prohibition has always been aimed – or selectively enforced – against minorities. To a great extent, the history of drug prohibition in the United States is a story of how the particular drugs used by the relatively powerless became progressively criminalized.[35] Long before the federal government began to regulate drug use, local ordinances in states like California criminalized those drugs preferred by poor immigrants. Today, racial bias is perhaps the most scandalous aspect of our punitive drug policy.

Contemporary statistics are shocking. Although whites and blacks are roughly comparable in their rates of illicit drug use, blacks are arrested, prosecuted, and punished for drug offenses far more frequently and harshly than whites. About 10 million whites and 2 million blacks are current users of illicit drugs. About five times more whites than blacks use marijuana, and about four times more whites than blacks use cocaine.

Whites outnumber blacks even in the case of crack, the illicit drug most commonly associated with minorities. In fact, most users of *any* illicit drug are white. But even though white drug users outnumber blacks by a five-to-one margin, blacks comprise 62.7 percent and whites 36.7 percent of all drug offenders admitted to state prisons. These racial disparities are significantly higher in some states than in others. In seven states, blacks represent more than 80 percent of all drug offenders sent to prison. In Maryland, blacks constitute 90 percent of all drug admissions. In Illinois, the state with the highest rate of black male drug offenders behind bars, a black man is fifty-seven times more likely to be sent to prison on drug charges than a white man.[36] Some of these disparities are a result of the objectionable practice of "racial profiling" the police practice of stopping, searching, and questioning criminal suspects solely on the basis of their race.

The notorious disparity in punishment for possession of powder and crack cocaine is the best evidence of racism in our drug policy. A first offender convicted of possessing more than five grams of crack receives a mandatory minimum of five years imprisonment. Five hundred grams of powder cocaine are needed before defendants receive a comparable sentence, thus creating the infamous hundred-to-one sentencing disparity. About 90 percent of federal crack defendants are black, while almost half of powder cocaine defendants are white. In 1995, the Sentencing Commission recommended that Congress re-evaluate the disparity in punishment between cocaine and crack, but both Houses of Congress rejected the Commission's advice. Shortly before leaving office, President Clinton recommended that this disparity be reduced. Tragically, it still persists in 2002.

Most commentators agree that these facts provide all of the proof we need of racism in our drug policy. Selective prohibition would have vanished long ago if whites had been sent to prison for drug offenses at the same rate as blacks. But a few thoughtful scholars disagree with these conclusions. Without contesting the data I have described, these experts insist that our drug policies are not racially biased. After all, it would be surprising if drug policy became more racist at the same time that our society generally, and our criminal justice system in particular, became less racist.

These scholars maintain that blacks are punished disproportionately to whites because of the special reasons to enforce criminalization more stringently in lower-class communities. Drugs are more devastating, they point out, in neighborhoods where people are struggling.

I have briefly responded to this school of thought in chapter 2, where I described the objectionable "compromise" of *enacting* criminal laws against drug use for everyone, while *enforcing* them more vigorously in poor communities. Here I make a different reply. Regardless of whether our drug policy can be defended as nondiscriminatory by criminal justice scholars, it is certainly *perceived* as racist by many minorities. Polls consistently reveal the tremendous split of opinion among whites and blacks about whether our legal system is just. The diametrically opposed reactions of whites and blacks to the verdict in the O.J. Simpson case illustrate this enormous racial gap. When drug laws are enforced most vigorously against blacks – even though they commit drug offenses at about the same frequency as whites – blacks come to believe that they are punished for what whites are allowed to do. This perception gives rise to a mistrust of law and disrespect for authority.

Attitudes about drug policy differ substantially in black and white communities. Many blacks suffer from the "dual frustration" of living with the problems associated with drugs in addition to the hardship created by tough enforcement of drug laws. Overall, blacks tend to have more negative opinions about drugs (both licit and illicit) than whites. At the same time, blacks are less likely than whites to believe that the solution to the problem is to enforce prohibition with severe punishments. Black mothers who are staunchly anti-drug are not enthusiastic about policies that lock up their sons and daughters for lengthy periods of time.

Repairing negative attitudes about law and authority among blacks is among the foremost challenges facing criminal justice policy in the twenty-first century. Ending prohibition would be a major step toward alleviating racism in the criminal law.

2. Health

In chapter 2, I critically examined the suggestion that prohibition is justified to protect health. Illicit drug use turns out not to be nearly as unhealthy as conventional wisdom would suggest – especially when compared to any number of recreational activities that have not been criminalized. Here, I describe several distinct ways that prohibition has had a pernicious impact on public health.

As we have seen, the National Institute on Drug Abuse lists over 25,000 fatalities from illicit drug use. But a majority of these deaths are more properly attributed to drug prohibition than to drug use. Some 14,300 fatalities are due to hepatitis and AIDS – diseases that are not caused by illicit drugs, but (mostly) by the dirty needles that heroin addicts tend to share. Needle exchange programs could prevent many of these fatalities. In fact, there may be no single innovation that could result in greater improvements in the health of illicit drug users. Researchers have consistently found that needle exchange programs reduce HIV transmission among those who inject drugs, as well as among their sexual partners and children. International organizations including the World Health Organization and the United Nations Program on HIV/AIDS have strongly supported the development of these programs throughout the world. In the United States, groups like the National Academy of Sciences and the American Medical Association favor efforts to improve access to sterile syringes. Many states and municipalities in the United States have followed these recommendations. But the possession, distribution, and sale of syringes remain criminal offenses in much of the country, and the federal government continues to prohibit the allocation of its funds for any needle exchange program.

Prohibition is destructive to health in a myriad of other respects. Since the vast majority of illicit drugs consumed for recreational purposes are bought on the street from unlicensed sellers, purchasers can have no confidence about what they are getting. Even sellers rarely know the exact contents of the substances they distribute. Street drugs may contain deadly impurities, and unknown potencies can contribute to overdose deaths. Admittedly, major progress in making drugs less dangerous would require decriminalization to extend beyond use to include production and sale. Enormous gains could result if state oversight of illicit drugs were comparable to the FDA's supervision of foods and licit drugs. We take for granted that the substances we consume contain only those ingredients that are listed on the labels. But illicit drugs are not subject to any quality controls.

Many sellers *do* know they are distributing something other than what the customer believes he is buying. Some experts fear that the recent increased penalties for ecstasy will lead to the production of counterfeit substances, so that distributors can meet the demand without risking the harsher sentences. DXM and PMA, which often are fraudulently sold as ecstasy, appear to be far more dangerous than the drug they replace. In March of 2001, the Federation of American Scientists (FAS) publicly opposed the increased punishments for ecstasy offenses, concluding that the sentences could be justified neither on pharmacological nor on policy grounds.

Health could be enhanced even if use alone were decriminalized. Recreational drug users with medical problems are reluctant to confide in their doctors, or to visit doctors at all. Pregnant women sometimes avoid prenatal care, worried that their babies will be taken away from them. When doctors are consulted, they often fail to provide all of the help they can. Surveys indicate that some 40 percent of pain specialists admit that they undermedicate patients to avoid the suspicion of the police. Their fears are warranted. Every year, approximately 100 doctors lose their licenses for prescribing narcotics. Doctors are put between a rock and a hard place; California juries have recently awarded huge damages to patients whose pain was insufficiently treated. But many patients attach so much stigma to the administration of opiates that they often prefer to suffer debilitating and demoralizing pain instead of seeking relief.

Moreover, according to what is sometimes called the *iron law of prohibition*, criminalization increases the potency of drugs. Since all illicit drug transactions must be concealed, both buyers and sellers have incentives to increase the purity of what they exchange. During the era of alcohol prohibition, beer was largely replaced by liquor. Since the end of that era, very potent liquors like grain alcohol have virtually disappeared from stores.

Today, diluted forms of illicit drugs – cocoa or opium teas, for example – are simply not available in black markets. Decriminalization would produce less potent mixtures of illicit drugs, which often reduce health risks to users.

Those who support our existing drug policy sometimes scoff at proposals to make drugs safer. Fewer health risks will simply induce more people to consume greater quantities of drugs. To discourage use, they contend, we must try to keep drugs as dangerous as possible. If people choose to break the law, they must accept the risk that their health will be jeopardized even more than they anticipate. What are we to think of such perverse attitudes? Why should we endorse policies that deliberately prevent illicit drugs from becoming safer? Surely *part* of the point of prohibition is to protect health. To the extent that prohibition actually makes drugs less safe, it undermines its very objective.

3. Foreign Policy

I cannot begin to summarize the vast historical evidence that demonstrates the pernicious role drugs have played in international affairs. The Opium Wars are perhaps the most notorious example of how attempts to prohibit the drug trade have led to conflict more harmful than drug use itself. The current war on drugs has come to resemble the Cold War, when governments with dismal records on human rights were befriended solely because of their opposition to Communism. Today, corrupt regimes are supported for no reason other than their alleged willingness to join the fight against drugs. For example, the United States sent millions of dollars to help the Taleban eradicate heroin. We will never know how much of this aid was diverted to finance the terrible acts of terrorism against our people.

The United Nations Single Convention on Narcotics Drugs, signed in 1961, was designed to foster an era of international cooperation by eliminating the cultivation, production, trade, and consumption of illicit substances throughout the world. By all accounts, this attempt has failed miserably. The United Nations estimates that the international drug business produces about 400 billion dollars each year – about the same amount as tourism. This figure exceeds the gross national product of 90 percent of the countries in the United Nations. In Mexico, for example, the value of the drug economy is almost twice as large as that of its oil exports – Mexico's largest legitimate industry. It is na ve to expect that a poor county whose best source of revenue is the illicit drug trade will choose to impoverish itself still more in a futile effort to help wealthy Americans become drug-free.

The real drug war, fought mostly on foreign soil, has caused the needless deaths of countless innocent civilians. In April of 2001, Peruvian jets shot down an unarmed Cessna, killing missionaries and their children. The money, equipment, training and intelligence for this mission were provided by the United States. After this tragedy, officials in the State Department expressed concerns that such incidents might lead the public to lose its resolve in the ongoing fight against drug traffickers around the world. Most of this war is waged in Colombia, the source of approximately 90 percent of the cocaine and most of the heroin that enters the United States. A five-year, 7.5 million dollar program – Plan Colombia – has been approved to help destroy Colombia's drug crops. Many experts predict that Plan Colombia will increase the instability and violence of the country's thirty-five-year-old civil war. South American neighbors have protested, anticipating an overflow of refugees and farmers. Almost all of the aid from the United States – which includes sixty attack helicopters – has been provided to Colombia's military and national police, despite their ongoing ties to violent right-wing paramilitary groups known to have killed thousands of civilians suspected of sympathizing with leftist guerrillas. In the summer of 2000, congressional opponents in the United States succeeded in making the aid contingent on President Pastrana's efforts to sever ties between his government and the right-wing paramilitaries. In the fall, however, President Clinton waived the conditions imposed by Congress in order to release the money to the Colombian military. By all indications, Plan Colombia has been escalated under President Bush.

In 1999, Congress passed the Western Hemisphere Drug Elimination Act, which authorized over 246 million dollars for eradication programs. These programs have exacerbated human rights violations, strengthened undemocratic governments, and helped to forge alliances between guerillas and peasant growers. Our allies are especially unhappy about the aerial spraying of coca crops; the European parliament voted 474 to 1 to oppose it. These interventions in Latin America have had a devastating impact on the environment. Eradication programs sponsored by the United States in Colombia have led to the clearing of over 1.75 million acres of Amazon rainforest. Colombia is the second most biodiverse country in the world, but drug war deforestation has led some environmentalists to predict that, within fifty years, its poor agricultural soils will be unable to support its population, plunging Colombia into the kind of famine seen in African countries like Somalia and Ethiopia. Meanwhile, aerial eradication has destroyed legal subsistence crops, and pesticides are blamed for a variety of health problems.

Perhaps we could understand how someone could turn a blind eye to these problems if Plan Colombia offered realistic prospects of success. But peasants and guerillas depend on profits from the drug trade, and the worsening economic conditions in Colombia decrease the likelihood that military intervention will succeed in reducing the quantity of drug crops produced. Eradication programs have consistently failed to curtail supplies in the United States because of the "push down, pop up" effect. Crops are more likely to be displaced than eliminated. For example, the massive eradication efforts in Bolivia and Peru throughout the mid-1990s caused production to shift to Colombia. Coca cultivation in Colombia doubled at the same time that Peru and Bolivia experienced 60 percent reductions. Cocoa has been cultivated in India, Indonesia and Taiwan; it could easily be grown in sub-Saharan Africa. Sometimes, production simply moves to the United States; at the turn of the twenty-first century, much and perhaps most of the marijuana consumed in this country is grown domestically. As I have indicated, economic realities suggest that effective curbs on production are unrealistic.

The annual drug certification process in the United States compounds many of these problems. According to this process, the State Department evaluates efforts made in foreign countries to combat drugs. A negative evaluation can result in economic sanctions and the withdrawal of foreign aid. Despite the recent increase in drug production in Colombia and Mexico, these countries were once again certified as cooperating with the objectives of drug policy in the United States. In fact, only two countries

– Afghanistan and Burma – are currently denied certification. This process has been the subject of intense criticism for years; the presidents of Colombia and Mexico said it "offends our countries" and dared to suggest that the United States be subjected to the same review it imposes on other countries. The certification process puts the burden of "winning" the drug war on producer nations, despite the fact that demand for illicit drugs within the United States is the driving force behind drug production abroad. Latin American leaders openly acknowledge that the drug war cannot be won without a reduction in demand in the United States.

Of course, punitive efforts within the United States to reduce demand are not the only alternative to our ineffective and destructive policies in Latin America. One option, advanced by Uruguayan President Jorge Batlle, would remove drugs from the black market, decreasing their price and the economic incentives to engage in drug trafficking. This strategy offers more realistic prospects of reducing the drug-related violence that continues to ravage Latin America. Closer to home, Mexican President Vicente Fox stunned the hemisphere by expressing his agreement with the legalization of drugs. Needless to say, neither Batlle's nor Fox's proposals were warmly received in the United States. Opposition from the most powerful country on earth continues to prevent foreign governments from devising more rational drug policies.

4. Crime

As we have seen, crime-prevention is one of the rationales most frequently offered on behalf of our punitive drug policy. Persons who use illicit drugs are more likely than abstainers to commit crimes. As we have also seen, however, not all defenders of prohibition subscribe to this rationale. Recall James Q. Wilson's remark: "It is not clear that enforcing the laws against drug use would reduce crime. On the contrary, crime may be caused by such enforcement."[37] We should remind ourselves of Wilson's reasoning. Drug prohibition increases systemic and economic crime. This is obvious in the case of systemic crime; violence is much more prevalent in illicit than in licit drug markets. The explanation of economic crime is a bit more controversial. Prohibition is somewhat effective in increasing the monetary price of drugs. Because drugs are expensive in black markets, they are often unaffordable to persons determined to get them. As a result, users generally and addicts in particular tend to commit economic crimes to obtain money to buy drugs. If drug sale were decriminalized, drugs would become cheaper, and users would be less likely to resort to theft to get the money to buy them. Therefore, decriminalizing sale would probably reduce the incidence of economic crime committed by drug users.

I suspect that Wilson is correct to speculate that drug prohibition is counterproductive in its impact on rates of crime. If we are interested in reducing crime, we have reason to prefer decriminalization to prohibition. In what follows, however, I will provide a different reason to believe that criminalization may actually cause more crime than it prevents. Conventional wisdom suggests that communities become safer when criminals are removed and sent to jail. Many believe this effect is magnified when drug users are incarcerated. Statistical evidence shows drug users to be the same kinds of people who are prone to commit crimes.

This conventional wisdom, however, has been challenged. Criminologists know that high rates of incarceration can backfire and make communities less safe in the long run. Eventually, criminals are returned to the neighborhoods from which they came. Prisons are schools for crime; offenders become more deeply immersed in criminal subcultures and learn more sophisticated skills for committing offenses. Men who have been incarcerated are less likely to marry, get good jobs, or to develop productive relationships with family members once they are back on the streets – all of which increase their propensity to commit crimes. Children from families with one parent in jail are significantly more likely to become criminals themselves – especially when their mothers are incarcerated. Those who have been jailed tend to hold unfavorable attitudes about the criminal justice system generally; prisons can embitter people and make them suspicious and disrespectful of authority. I have already mentioned the negative attitudes in black communities about our system of criminal justice. This lack of confidence among minorities in our legal system is costly. A wealth of data indicates that respect and trust in legal institutions is far more effective in producing compliance with law than threats of punishment.

An additional factor leads criminologists to believe that punishing drug sellers increases crime. This offense, unlike most others, is fully *replaceable*. If a burglar is incarcerated, there will be one less burglar in the neighborhood. But if a drug seller is incarcerated, there will be just as many drug sellers as before. The removal of a dealer from the streets provides an opportunity for others to capture his share of the market. When the seller is in prison, no reduction in the quantity of drugs exchanged is likely to take place. And when the original seller returns from prison, we should not expect him to become a model citizen. The net effect on crime is likely to be greater than before he was punished.

Prohibiting drug use is probably counterproductive because of the sheer scale of incarceration and the existence of viable alternatives. To appreciate how massive rates of punishment can increase crime, we must understand why some neighborhoods suffer from high rates of crime, while others do not. Many studies indicate that criminality is strongly affected by the presence or absence of social organizations in communities. In particular, neighborhoods in which parents collectively share the responsibility for supervising children and teens are less likely to experience high rates of crime. In the long run, the social organizations that prevent serious crime are disrupted by policies that incarcerate large numbers of community members for substantial periods of time. When many people are sent to prison, neighborhoods can reach a "tipping point" at which they become destabilized. Communities are deprived of the group of people who, as young adults, would soon be likely to form organizations to produce order. By disrupting the formation of social organizations that protect communities, punitive policies may actually cause more crime than they prevent.

Apart from the sheer scale of incarceration brought about by prohibition, how do the foregoing considerations provide any special reason to favor the decriminalization of drugs? Isn't the above argument an indictment of our entire system of criminal justice? The answer is that few realistic options other than prison exist for violent criminals. As I have argued, however, recreational drug users need not be punished at all. The reasons in favor of criminalization justify neither the hardship for drug users themselves, nor the losses for the communities from which they come.

5. Lies and Hypocrisy

Truth is among the casualties of our misguided drug policy. The demonization of illicit drugs is so pervasive that frank and honest discourse is all but impossible. Policies are implemented and continued not because they are believed to be effective, but because people are afraid of the repercussions if they are changed. Politics and hysteria, not science and sound principles, continue to fuel our drug policy.

We should be especially dismayed when lies and distortions masquerade as drug education. Students have a right to expect that they will be told the truth in their classrooms. Polls indicate that a majority of students do not believe what they are taught in their drug education programs in schools.[38] Their skepticism gives rise to at least two problems. First, some drugs like methamphetamine (speed) may really be quite harmful when used recreationally. If so, however, users would be unlikely to heed the warnings, since they are accustomed to exaggerated claims about even the safest illicit drugs. Moreover, students who know that they are exposed to propaganda in the guise of education can hardly be expected to have favorable attitudes about school in general. Mistrust of these programs nurtures an adversarial and confrontational attitude toward teachers. It is hard to estimate the extent to which students have become cynical of education generally because of the nonsense to which they have been subjected in the name of drug education.

Educators themselves often share the negative opinions of their students. But many are reluctant to dismantle deceitful programs because of the pressure to "do something" about the drug problem. Mayor Ross Anderson of Salt Lake City has recently decided to sever the city's involvement with Drug Abuse Resistance Education (DARE) that had been adopted in some 10,000 school districts across the United States. After studying the available evidence, Ross concluded that DARE programs were "a complete fraud" and have "actually done a lot of harm." Most empirical studies indicate that schoolchildren who had been exposed to DARE programs were no less likely to use drugs later in life than those who had not. Still, Anderson said that his position had caused a furor. Leaders who decide to terminate even ineffective and counterproductive anti-drug programs are often tarnished as "soft on drugs."

Curiously, drug education programs are often designed and led by individuals who are notorious for their admitted inability to use drugs sensibly. These individuals relate powerful anecdotes about the depths to which their heavy drug abuse had caused them to sink before they reformed and became abstinent. We should be baffled by the employment of such people in drug education programs. If we wanted to find an educator to teach students about investments, we would not select someone who had lost all of his money in the stock market. If we wanted to find an educator to teach students about studying, we would not select someone who had never passed a course in school. Why do drug education programs seek the most extreme and pathetic drug abusers for their supposed expertise? Unfortunately, students exposed to such programs are forced to look elsewhere for reliable information about drugs.

Occasionally, drug policies outside the United States are somewhat less hypocritical. The recent move in England to reclassify cannabis from class B to class C was designed to make drug offenses more "credible." More and more politicians confessed to having tried cannabis, although few admitted to having enjoyed it. As a result, no one could continue to pretend that marijuana is especially dangerous. Rates of cannabis use have climbed in England, and 58 percent of all respondents aged fifteen and over oppose criminal penalties for possession. Support for decriminalization is especially strong among those under thirty-four, with more than two-thirds in favor. Since credibility is at issue, England is reconsidering its stringent punishments of ecstasy as well. Over half a million English people take ecstasy each weekend, and its present status as a class A drug has done little to discourage use. Credibility is indeed necessary if the criminal justice is to operate smoothly. Still, I have defended a better reason to reclassify drugs like cannabis and ecstasy. Criminalization was never justified in the first place.

6. Civil Liberties

Prohibition has eroded precious civil liberties in which Americans take pride. Many legal theorists speak openly of the "drug exception" to the

Bill of Rights. Since illicit drugs are easy to conceal and involve consensual transactions that frequently occur behind closed doors, police have been forced to resort to unusual and objectionable tactics to enforce prohibition. For example, criminalization accounts for a majority of authorized wiretaps in the United States. Judicial approval of many of these tactics has led to a tremendous expansion of police power. To be sure, the era of alcohol prohibition also required law enforcement to be ingenious and creative. But the lack of sympathy for alcohol prohibition among the judiciary helps to explain why a number of civil liberties (such as the defense of entrapment) were actually expanded during that period. Today, the judiciary expresses fewer reservations about the objectives of drug prohibition. Even Thurgood Marshall, perhaps the best-known liberal on the Supreme Court in the latter half of the twentieth century, remarked: "If it's a dope case, I won't even read the petition. I ain't giving no break to no dope dealer."[39]

Every year, many of the most important issues decided by the Supreme Court involve criminal procedure. A high percentage of these cases test the constitutional boundaries of enforcing drug prohibitions. Consider a handful of the legal questions resolved in 2001. Should police be allowed to employ sophisticated thermal-imaging devices to scan homes to identify persons who might be growing marijuana in their basements? Can drivers be stopped at random so that drug-sniffing dogs can go through their cars? May a homeowner be prevented from entering his house for two hours while the police obtain a warrant to search for drugs? Can students be barred from extracurricular activities because they refuse to take drug tests? May a hospital secretly test the urine of selected pregnant women for cocaine and provide the results to the police for prosecution? These examples represent the tip of the iceberg; courts wrestle with issues like these each term. We can anticipate that the kinds of issues to be decided in the next term, and the term after that, will be very similar. Often, but not always, judges decide these cases by ruling against drug defendants and in favor of law enforcement. Each such decision narrows our freedoms and expands the power of the state. We should all be worried about this trend. Freedoms sacrificed in drug cases are lost in other kinds of cases as well, diminishing the civil liberties of all citizens.

In the past decade, asset forfeiture has been a favorite strategy in the fight against illicit drugs. This tactic allows the state to seize cash, cars, homes, and any other property believed to be used in illegal activity. Adverse publicity surrounding the abuse of forfeiture law led Congress to regulate it more stringently in 2000. But the new restrictions only affect seizures under federal law; significant abuses continue at the local level. Municipal police departments still "police for profit," using asset forfeiture to finance new buildings, squad cars, and equipment.

Prohibition has eroded civil liberties around the world. Consider only one of many such examples. For a decade, drug-trafficking cases in Colombia have routinely been sent to special tribunals that allow judges, prosecutors and witnesses to remain anonymous. These "faceless courts" have survived, despite protests by the United Nations and human rights organizations that they violate international law. The United States is the only country to approve of these courts – which clearly would be unconstitutional if used at home – because of our desire to stem the flow of illicit drugs across our borders.

I have already commented how drug prohibitions have given rise to "racial profiling" by law enforcement – a practice by which persons are stopped and detained because of the color of their skin. Most Americans recognize this practice to be wrong and unjust, and President Bush has promised to curtail it. But racial profiling is not easily separated from our punitive drug policy. Police who stop drivers on highways because of their race are almost always searching for drugs. When a law is enacted that makes criminals of over twenty million Americans, it is naïve to expect it to be enforced in a fair and even-handed way. Such laws are bound to give rise to selective enforcement. Not surprisingly, the least powerful members of our society bear the brunt of law enforcement. Anyone who is serious about ending racial profiling should be receptive to the repeal of prohibition. We must be critical of laws that can only be enforced by eroding our civil liberties.

7. Corruption

There may be no greater threat to the rule of law than corruption and abuse of authority among government officials. Prohibition and the huge amounts of money in the illicit drug trade create irresistible temptations for law-enforcement agents to place themselves above the law. The United Nations Drug Control Program noted the inevitable risk of drug-related police corruption in 1998, reporting that "wherever there is a well-organized, illicit drug industry, there is also the danger of corruption." This danger is especially grave in drug-producing countries throughout the world. But no one should underestimate the extent of corruption in the United States.

The amount of corruption is impossible to measure with any precision. Some studies claim to conservatively estimate that 30 percent of the nation's police officers have been unlawfully involved with illicit drugs since becoming employed in law enforcement. According to the Government Accounting Office, half of all police officers in FBI-led corruption cases between 1993 and 1997 were convicted of drug-related offenses. Serious criminal activities perpetrated by on-duty police included stealing money and/or drugs from drug dealers, selling stolen drugs, protecting drug operations, committing perjury, and submitting false crime reports. The Mollen Commission, appointed to investigate corruption in the New York City Police Department, made similar findings. It identified police corruption, brutality, and violence in *every* high-crime precinct with an active narcotics trade. The Commission noted many patterns of police corruption and brutality, including stealing from drug dealers, engaging in unlawful searches, seizures and car stops, dealing and using drugs, lying in order to justify unlawful searches and arrests and to forestall complaints of abuse, and indiscriminate beating of innocent and guilty alike. Although profit was the primary motive for drug-related police corruption, the Mollen Commission identified power and vigilante justice as two additional factors.

Corruption in law enforcement will never be eliminated. But it is hard to think of a single step that would be more helpful in limiting opportunities for corruption than the repeal of selective drug prohibition.

8. Money

The eighth and final counterproductive effect of selective prohibition I will mention is the easiest to understand – so I will deal with it quickly. Our punitive drug policies cost exorbitant amounts of money. The federal government now spends close to 20 billion dollars per year, and state and local governments at least that much again, on combating illegal drugs. Most of this money has been wasted. If we stopped punishing drug users, taxpayers would reap enormous savings.

Of course, decriminalization of drug production and sale would bring about additional financial rewards. Illicit drugs are big business; marijuana may be the biggest cash crop in the United States today. If decriminalized, this massive industry would finally become subject to taxation. Where should the money be spent? Many who are critical of our punitive policy are quick to answer that the money should be invested in drug treatment. At the present time, 31 percent of the federal drug budget is spent on treatment and prevention, while 69 percent is allocated to law enforcement and interdiction. According to the White House, only 40 percent of addicts who need treatment receive it. Later in this chapter I will express skepticism about drug treatment, at least when it is mandatory. Education is my favorite candidate for increased funding. State universities – the most important vehicle for upward mobility in our country – periodically face budget crises because of their competition for tax dollars that are used to finance prohibition. But there is no reason to decide exactly how to spend the savings from decriminalization. I simply point out that the money could be used for any number of valuable purposes. *Any* use of these revenues would be preferable to paying for unjust punishments.

I have provided a very brief sketch of eight respects in which our punitive drug policy is counterproductive and detrimental to us all – drug users and non-users alike. We might disagree about whether I have overlooked a particular effect that is more worrisome than those I have discussed. Or we can quibble about whether I have exaggerated or distorted the evidence in one example or another. In combination, however, these allegations provide a powerful indictment of prohibition. No reasonable person can dismiss each of these problems as insignificant and unimportant. Those who continue to support the punishment of illicit drug users may respond by pointing out that any war – including the war on drugs – will exact a terrible price. That price, however, must be worth paying. No policy should be continued unless its objective is sufficiently important to justify the collateral damage we know has occurred and have every reason to believe will continue to occur. What *is* that important objective? I have argued that there is no good answer to this basic question – no adequate justification for punishing people simply for using (some) drugs for recreational purposes. The injustice to drug users is not the only reason to oppose prohibition.

THE WORLD OF DECRIMINALIZED DRUGS

No sensible person can react with indifference to the foregoing allegations. Surely we should be alarmed about the several respects in which our drug policy is counterproductive – even if we are unmoved by the injustice of prohibition. How can anyone support the status quo in light of the problems I have raised? The answer is clear. Prohibitionists believe that we must continue to criminalize drug use because the alternative would be disastrous. If we did *not* punish drug use, the number of recreational drug users would skyrocket. According to James Q. Wilson, "the central problem with legalizing drugs is that it will increase drug consumption under almost any reasonable guess." His own guess is that "consumption will go up dramatically."[40] William Bennett echoes this sentiment. He writes: "Americans feel up to their hips in drugs now. They would be up to their necks under legalization."[41] President Bush concurs, saying "drug legalization would be a social catastrophe. Drug use and addiction would soar."[42]

We have already encountered this prediction – on several occasions. Recall the tragic story of Sue Miller, related in the first section of chapter 1. I asked how her plight could possibly hope to persuade us to retain the very policies that led to her death. The answer, of course, is that criminalization is needed to prevent other people from succumbing to the evils of drugs. Many prohibitionists are convinced that we must continue to punish drug users because the failure to do so would create too many Sue Millers. Are they correct? No assessment of our drug policy can be complete unless we try to answer this question. We must attempt to describe what our society would be like if the recreational use of illicit drugs were decriminalized. In particular, we must ask how the repeal of criminal penalties for use would affect drug consumption. In the minds of many thinkers, this is the major question – and perhaps the only question – on which the justifiability of our punitive drug policy depends.

The specter of escalating drug use is so worrisome that many prohibitionists are led to reject even the most modest and sensible changes in our criminal laws. The controversy about medical marijuana provides an excellent example. Politicians who continue to forbid doctors to prescribe marijuana rarely complain that it has no legitimate medical use. After all, they are not doctors; on what basis *could* they challenge licensed physicians who believe that marijuana is effective in treating diseases like glaucoma, leukemia, and multiple sclerosis? More typically, politicians reject the use of marijuana for medical purposes because they believe it represents the "camel's nose under the tent." In other words, allowing marijuana to be used for medical purposes would begin the irreversible descent down the slippery slope toward wholesale decriminalization and an eventual explosion in marijuana consumption. Apparently, the risks of greater marijuana use are sufficiently troublesome to justify withholding effective medicine from sick patients. Those who advocate marijuana as medicine make a variety of distinct replies to this concern. Can the rationale for criminalization possibly be so urgent that the sick must be condemned to suffer? Wouldn't a prohibitionist be quick to make an exception on behalf of his own family if the medical need arose? Would he really allow his own mother to suffer, knowing that an existing substance could ease her pain? These questions are not so hard to answer. At some point, however, we should move beyond these easy issues and confront the worst fears of prohibitionists directly. What would happen if illicit drugs like marijuana were decriminalized? We must endeavor to picture the world of decriminalized drugs. We must try to imagine what our society would be like if we stopped punishing people simply for using drugs for recreational purposes.

Of course, predictions that decriminalization would cause an escalation in rates of drug use cannot really be the complete rationale for punishing drug users. These fears do not belong alongside worries about children, crime, health, and immorality – each of which was discussed in chapter 2. The concern I have mentioned in this section is only a step toward a justification of criminalization. No one contends that we should punish drug use simply because the failure to do so will result in greater numbers of drug users; we must be given an additional reason to believe that the anticipated increase would be bad. This additional reason, then, completes the story and converts this prediction into a rationale for prohibition. An increase in the number of drug users might be thought to be bad for any of the four reasons discussed in chapter 2. The increase might be worse for children, cause crime, undermine health, and/or contribute to immorality. Daniel Lungren, former Attorney General of California, offers an expanded litany of concerns. He writes: "I don't think that you can argue against the fact that the costs in homelessness, unemployment, welfare, lost productivity, disability payments, school dropouts, lawsuits, medical care costs, chronic mental illness, accidents, crime, child abuse, and child neglect would all increase if we in fact legalized drugs."[43]

Lungren's comments suggest that he believes prohibition "works." But it is hard to interpret the existing data as evidence for the effectiveness of criminalization. Recall some of the sobering statistics. Hundreds of billions of dollars on law enforcement expended over dozens of years have not had an obvious impact on the demand for illicit drugs or the difficulty of obtaining them. About 80 or 90 million living Americans have experimented with illicit drugs at some time in their lives. Every day, about 6,400 Americans try marijuana for the first time. Illicit drugs remain easy to find. In 1999, 90 percent of high-school seniors reported that marijuana was fairly easy or very easy to obtain; 44 percent said the same about cocaine, and 32 percent said the same about heroin. The street price of most illicit drugs has fallen since 1980 – sometimes dramatically – indicating that quantities remain abundant.

Of course, we should never assume that things cannot get worse. Prohibitionists insist that punishment is needed to keep the problem from growing completely out of control. This concern must be taken seriously.

In what follows, I will argue that we have no basis for confidence in our prediction about how drug use, and the problems associated with it, would vary in a world in which people were no longer punished for using illicit drugs. Here as, elsewhere, anecdotes tend to masquerade as evidence. Speculation is rife; people offer bold conjectures about how a change in the law would affect behavior. Perhaps we can anticipate how people would react the day after prohibition is repealed. But how about the next month? Or the next year? Or the next several years? I will contend that all predictions about the medium- and long-term effects of decriminalization should be taken with a large grain of salt. I will describe several reasons why no credible forecast can be made about rates of consumption in a world in which drug use for recreational purposes has been decriminalized.

We should begin by offering a somewhat more detailed sketch of the concerns that lead many thoughtful people to support our existing drug policy. According to this train of thought, illicit drugs are extraordinarily powerful. Although millions of people succumb to their allure, the high cost of drugs is the single most important factor that keeps consumption within reasonable bounds. Decriminalization would reduce the monetary cost of drugs. Even more importantly, decriminalization would eliminate the non-monetary cost of drugs – the fear of arrest and prosecution. Lower the monetary cost and remove the threat of punishment, and the incidence of drug use will grow exponentially.

One response to this prediction would question the connection between monetary cost and the incidence of drug use. According to the Drug Enforcement Administration (DEA), the retail price of cocaine dropped from 158 dollars per gram in 1990 to between sixty and eighty dollars in 2001. Since the number of cocaine users in the United Sates has been relatively stable throughout the last decade – at about 1.5 million – price may not be a crucial variable in estimating future consumption. I concede, however, that use and monetary price must be connected to *some* degree. Therefore, a better response to this prediction would begin by challenging the claim that decriminalization will cause the monetary price of drugs to plummet. Admittedly, most illicit drugs are relatively inexpensive to produce, and tend to be costly to consumers largely because sellers demand enormous profits in order to justify the risks they must take. But why assume that decriminalization will make illicit drugs significantly more affordable? Decriminalization itself, as I have emphasized, need not allow illicit drugs to be sold with impunity. Suppose that use is permitted, but sale is punished. If removing the threat of punishment stimulates demand, as prohibitionists tend to assume, basic principles of economics would suggest that the price of drugs would *rise* rather than fall. Clearly, this cannot be what defenders of the status quo have in mind when they forecast disaster. What system of production do they imagine when they try to estimate the cost of drugs in a world of decriminalization? Do they suppose that illicit drugs will be bought and sold like alcohol and tobacco? Perhaps. But decriminalization itself makes no such suppositions. Surely the question of what cocaine and heroin (for example) would cost in a world of decriminalization depends on questions that decriminalization itself does not purport to answer – questions about how illicit drugs will be produced and sold.

Suppose, however, that we decide to move beyond decriminalization as I have defined it here, and no longer criminalize the sale of illicit drugs. Some system of lawful distribution would have to be implemented. Suppose that the system governing the sale of alcohol and tobacco were used as a model. How would this system affect the monetary cost of illicit drugs? The answer to this question depends mostly on two factors. First, decriminalization of sale would suddenly make illicit drugs subject to taxation. States that already levy sizeable sales taxes on alcohol and tobacco would certainly impose high sales taxes on illicit drugs as well. The amount of this tax is hard to estimate, and would vary from place to place. States would be expected to impose a tax that is sufficiently high to discourage consumption. But taxes could not be too high. Many of the advantages of decriminalizing the sale of illicit drugs would disappear if high taxes caused the reappearance of a black market. I will not try to estimate the optimal rate of taxation. Whatever the exact figure, we can be sure that taxes would add significantly to the price of newly decriminalized drugs.

The second factor affecting the price of decriminalized illicit drugs is even more difficult to estimate. If illicit drugs are anywhere near as harmful as many people believe, some mechanism must be created to compensate victims for the harms they suffer when drugs are used. Roughly, these harms might be of two kinds. First, drug users might harm themselves. Like smokers of tobacco, illicit drug users might make more frequent visits to doctors and hospitals. Second, drug users might harm others. Like drinkers of alcohol, illicit drug users might cause more accidents. One way to compensate victims for each of these kinds of harms is by allowing lawsuits against producers of illicit drugs. We have been reluctant to allow such lawsuits in the cases of tobacco and alcohol; powerful lobbies have fought against them for years. But we need not be so reluctant when we establish a new system of sale for illicit drugs. Producers could be made to pay for the costs of the various harms that their customers cause to themselves and to others. Producers would be able to pay these costs, and remain in business, only if they could pass them along to buyers by raising their prices. How much of an increase in price would be needed to compensate all of the victims for the harms they suffer when illicit drugs are used? No one knows.

Of course, we cannot begin to answer this question unless we know how dangerous illicit drugs really are. I have claimed that the dangers of illicit drugs tend to be exaggerated. Even if I am mistaken about the dangers of illicit drugs today, we can be confident that illicit drugs would be less dangerous in a world in which production and sale had been decriminalized. In such a world, suppliers would have enormous incentives to make their drugs as safe as possible in order to limit the amount of money they would be required to pay when harm is caused by the use of their product. If a given drug is very dangerous, we might even find that no company could hope to make a profit by selling it, and the drug would disappear from the lawful market. We simply do not know how dangerous illicit drugs will turn out to be in a world of decriminalization; to this point, producers have had no motivation to improve the safety of their products. But financial incentives are bound to make illicit drugs safer. Therefore, we do not know how much this factor will affect the cost of illicit drugs.

As a result of these two factors, we have almost no basis for estimating how the monetary price of decriminalized drugs would differ from their price in today's black market. We do not know how much states will decide to tax the sale of drugs. In addition, we do not know how much sellers will have to charge in order to survive when lawsuits are brought against them. If this latter figure is high, drugs will be expensive, and fears about cheap drugs would be put to rest. But if this figure is low, the price of drugs would decrease. But if the amount sellers must charge as a result of these lawsuits is low, it means that drugs turned out to be less dangerous than we thought. If drugs are not as dangerous as we thought, we will come to wonder why we were so worried about making them more affordable in the first place. The general point is clear. Those who tend to trust the pricing mechanisms of the market should not assume that these mechanisms will fail in the case of illicit drugs. At the very least, we should not assume that dangerous illicit drugs would suddenly become cheap in a world of decriminalization.

However uncertain we may be about how decriminalization will affect the monetary cost of drugs, it will clearly eliminate the non-monetary cost – the fear of arrest and prosecution. To the extent that this fear has helped to keep illicit drug use in check, we would anticipate that decriminalization would cause the incidence of drug use to rise. But to what extent? How will consumption change in a world in which drug users are not worried about punishment? No one knows; no single piece of evidence on this point is compelling. But several reasons conspire to suggest that the threat of punishment is not especially effective in curbing drug use. In what follows, I will describe a number of reasons to doubt that the removal of criminal penalties would cause a significant increase in the use of illicit drugs.

One source of evidence is obtained through various kinds of surveys. People who have never used drugs are asked to explain their reasons for abstaining, and to speculate about how their willingness to experiment would be affected by a change in the law. Very few respondents cite fear of punishment as a substantial factor in their decision not to try drugs. The more dangerous the drug is perceived to be, the smaller the number of respondents who mention the law when asked to explain their reluctance to use it. Virtually no non-users say that they would begin to use heroin, for example, if the fear of criminal liability were removed. Other surveys ask former users why they decided to quit. Those who once used drugs are asked why they don't continue to do so today, and to explain why their behavior has changed. Very few respondents report that fear of arrest and prosecution led them to stop using drugs. They cite a bad experience with a drug, or some new responsibility like a job or a newborn – but rarely mention the risk of punishment. Of course, the value of these kinds of surveys is questionable. We may doubt that people have accurate insights into why they behave as they do, or what might lead them to change their behavior. Surely, however, these surveys provide better evidence than mere conjecture. These (easily replicated) surveys suggest that the fear of punishment is not a major factor in explaining why drug use is not more pervasive than it is.

What other evidence is relevant in deciding how the fear of punishment affects the incidence of drug use? We might examine how trends in illicit drug use over the past thirty years are correlated with changes in law enforcement. If the fear of punishment were a significant factor in deterring illicit drug use, one would expect that rates of consumption would decline as punishments increased in frequency and severity. For the most part, however, there is no correlation between the frequency and severity of punishment and trends in drug use. If we look at the decade from 1980 to 1990, a case could be made that punishments were effective in deterring use. The incidence of illicit drug use, which peaked in 1979, steadily decreased throughout the 1980s. But frequent and severe punishments have not caused further declines during the 1990s; drug use has remained relatively flat in the past decade. We reach the same conclusion when we examine the data on a state-by-state basis. States with greater rates of incarceration for drug offenders tend to experience higher, not lower rates of drug use. Prohibitionists who predict a massive increase in drug use in a world of decriminalization must struggle to explain these data. If punitive drug policies are needed to keep drug use in check, why do actual trends in drug consumption prove so resistant to the massive efforts we have made to punish drug users?

Additional evidence can be gleaned from the experience of other countries, where the fear of arrest and prosecution for the use of given drugs is practically nonexistent. Most countries have lower rates of illicit drug use, even though given drugs are higher in quality, lower in price, and less likely to result in punishments. American teenagers consume more mari-juana and other illicit drugs than their European counterparts (although European teens are more likely to smoke cigarettes and drink alcohol). Consider the Netherlands, known for its relatively permissive drug laws. In Amsterdam, marijuana is used with impunity in licensed coffee shops. The border town of Venlo has opened two drive-through marijuana and hashish outlets to cater to German "drug tourists." Despite the lax attitude among the Dutch, illicit drug use is less widespread than in the United States. Although marijuana prevalence rates are roughly comparable in the two countries, about twice as many residents of the United States have experimented with other kinds of illicit drugs. In general, data from other parts of the world provide better evidence for an inverse than for a posi-tive correlation between severities of punishments and rates of illicit drug use. Admittedly, however, this evidence is inconclusive. No country in the world has implemented decriminalization as I have defined it here. Even in Portugal, which has perhaps the least punitive drug policy in the world, illicit substances are confiscated and those who possess them are often required to undergo treatment.

The history of the United States provides further reason to doubt that fear of punishment plays a major role in reducing the use of illicit drugs. We must keep in mind that, for all practical purposes, drug prohibition did not begin until the early part of the twentieth century. In the nine-teenth century, purchases of opium, morphine, cocaine and marijuana were subject to almost no restrictions. Americans could buy these drugs in many different varieties from many different sources – including by mail order. But even though criminal penalties were not imposed for the use of opiates and cocaine, these drugs were far less popular than alcohol and tobacco today. Admittedly, however, the verdict of history is mixed. Most Americans agree that our era of alcohol prohibition was a dismal failure. By most accounts, however, per capita consumption of alcohol decreased throughout prohibition, and did not return to pre-prohibition levels for many years. This finding has led some social scientists to conclude that prohibition "worked" after all – if a reduction in use is the most important criterion of success. Curiously, however, even those social scientists who insist that alcohol prohibition was effective almost never recommend that our country should reinstate that policy. In any event, we must remember that the consumption of alcohol decreased from 1920 to 1933 even though the state did not punish possession in the home – or even the purchase of alcohol. If prohibition worked, it achieved its success without resorting to the extreme measure of putting drinkers in jail.

Trends in the use of *licit* drugs provide yet another source of evidence. Prohibitionists tend to point to a reduction in illicit drug use over the last twenty years as a reason to believe that severe punishments have been effective in curbing drug use. Comparable declines in the use of alcohol and tobacco, however, have taken place over this same period of time – even without the threat of criminal liability. Rates of monthly illicit drug use in the United States peaked at about 14 percent in 1979, steadily declined to a low of just above 5 percent in 1992, and slowly increased thereafter to about 6 percent in 1999. Trends in alcohol and tobacco use exhibit more similarities than dissimilarities with these patterns. The overall use of alcohol and tobacco declined throughout the 1980s, and rebounded somewhat during the 1990s. We have ample evidence that the use of licit drugs can be decreased without the need to resort to criminal sanctions. We should probably assume that the same is true of illicit drugs.

If changes in the certainty and severity of punishment are not major factors in explaining trends in illicit drug use, what *does* account for these patterns? This is one of the most fascinating and difficult questions about drug use, and I confess to having no good answer to it. Trends in the use of both licit and illicit drugs are as baffling and mysterious as trends in fashion. Unless we have better theories to explain why people use drugs, our forecasts about the future are bound to be simplistic. No one has a convincing explanation of why the use of a given drug increases or decreases within a given group in a given place at a given time. By 2001, the popularity of crack in inner cities had waned enormously. Crack is no longer regarded as "cool" and "hip." Why? No simple answer can be given. Most experts believe that a heightened consciousness about health contributed to the reduction in the use of licit drugs during the 1980s. But what caused this growing concern about health – and why did it not lead rates of drug use to fall still further throughout the 1990s? Again, no answer is clearly correct. But credibility is strained if we suppose that a factor is important in accounting for decreases in the consumption of alcohol and tobacco, but is unimportant in accounting for decreases in the consumption of illicit drugs – especially when the patterns of these decreases are roughly comparable. We have little reason to believe that punishments play a central role in accounting for trends in drug use.

I have provided several reasons to doubt that punishment is needed to keep rates of illicit drug use within reasonable bounds. But skepticism about the efficacy of punishment as a deterrent to drug use is only a small part of the reason why predictions are so tenuous in a world of decriminalized drugs. Recall the meaning of decriminalization. The only change that this policy requires is that the state would not *punish* anyone simply for using a drug for recreational purposes. The state can adopt any number of devices to discourage drug use, as long as these devices are not punitive. In chapter 1, I indicated that legal philosophers disagree about which kinds of state responses should be categorized as modes of punishment. In particular, drug *treatment*, even when mandatory, is not always regarded as a kind of punishment. I am inclined to believe that mandatory treatment *is* a mode of punishment, and therefore is incompatible with decriminalization as I define it here. But perhaps I am mistaken. If mandatory treatment is *not* a kind of punishment, the state may require that recreational drug users undergo treatment. Clearly, mandatory treatment has the potential to make a huge impact on rates of drug use in a world of decriminalization. To estimate the size of this impact, we would need to assess the efficacy of treatment in reducing the incidence of drug use. Obviously, enormous controversy surrounds this issue. Decriminalization itself does not determine whether treatment will be mandated (assuming that treatment is not a mode of punishment), or whether mandated treatment will be successful. Therefore, we have no firm basis to predict how rates of drug use will change in a world of decriminalization.

Moreover, as I have indicated, many institutions other than the state can (and do) play a significant role in discouraging drug use. In a world of decriminalization, some of these institutions might exert even more influence. Private businesses, schools, insurance companies, and universities, to cite a few examples, might adopt policies that discriminate against users of licit or illicit drugs. Suppose that employers fired or denied promotions to workers who use cocaine. Suppose that schools barred students who drink alcohol from participating in extracurricular activities. Suppose that insurance companies charged higher premiums to policy holders who smoke tobacco. Suppose that college loans and grants were withdrawn from undergraduates who use marijuana. I do not endorse any of these ideas; many seem unwise and destined to backfire. Removing drug-using kids from schools, for example, is likely to increase their consumption. I simply point out that these institutions could have a far greater impact on decisions to use drugs than the threat of criminal punishment.

Predictions about drug use in a world of decriminalization are confounded by yet another phenomenon – the "forbidden fruit" effect. Many people – adolescents in particular – are attracted to an activity precisely *because* it is forbidden or perceived as dangerous. Much of the thrill of illicit drug use stems from its illegality and the culture of deviance that surrounds it. This phenomenon was evident from 1920 to 1933, when the consumption of alcohol was glorified as a form of social protest. And the forbidden fruit effect may be even more prominent today, as adolescents continue to smoke tobacco despite massive efforts to persuade them to quit. If we change the law, the appeal of illicit drugs will be changed as well. But to what extent? Might the use of some illicit drugs actually decrease because they are no longer forbidden? No one knows. Although many scholars have noted the forbidden fruit effect, serious research has yet to demonstrate its real significance. Undoubtedly, some people who would have become heavy users had drugs remained illegal would abstain if their use were decriminalized. But we can only guess at how many such people exist. In a world of decriminalization, the impact of the forbidden fruit phenomenon on the long-term incidence of illicit drug use remains unclear.

Predictions about future use invariably assume that the drugs of tomorrow will resemble the drugs of today. This assumption seems extraordinarily naïve. The development of new and different substances makes predictions about consumption enormously speculative. Even though many illicit drugs – heroin and LSD, for example – were originally created by pharmaceutical companies, reputable corporations have tried hard to disassociate their substances from illicit drugs. But decriminalization may lead pharmaceutical companies to change their priorities in research and development. To date, these companies have not expended their talent or ingenuity to create better and safer recreational drugs. One can only wonder about the products that might be developed if the best minds were put to the task. If more enjoyable and less dangerous drugs could be perfected, consumption may boom. But the development of better and safer drugs would make the increase in consumption less of a social problem.

Whether or not new drugs appear on the market, no one can predict how users will substitute newly decriminalized drugs for existing licit drugs. In a world of decriminalization, consumers would have lawful alternatives that we generally take for granted in other contexts. Users would not have to worry about punishment in attempts to learn which kinds of drugs they prefer. Over time, one would expect that users would gravitate toward those drugs that could be integrated into their lifestyles most easily. Presumably, this tendency accounts for why marijuana is far and away the most widely used illicit drug in the United States and England today. Marijuana is correctly perceived to be less dangerous, and more easily assimilated into daily activities, than other illicit drugs.

If decriminalization would facilitate substitution among drugs, we have a ready reply to one answer that drug prohibitionists often give when challenged to defend different policies toward licit and illicit drugs. This challenge is familiar: Why should we punish users of marijuana and cocaine, while permitting the use of alcohol and tobacco? Many attempts to answer this question have been made; none is persuasive. Here, however, I want to examine one particular answer that is given frequently. Prohibitionists typically concede – as they must – that alcohol and tobacco cause tremendous social harm. Why, they ask, should we compound the problem by decriminalizing other drugs that are socially harmful as well? As far as I can see, this response does not meet the challenge as much as evade it. It does not even attempt to identify a relevant dissimilarity between those drugs we should allow and those drugs we should prohibit. More importantly for present purposes, this reply seemingly assumes that the decriminalization of illicit drugs will simply add to the total amount of harm already caused by licit drugs like alcohol and tobacco. In other words, the consumption of these licit drugs would be unchanged, so any growth in the consumption of illicit drugs caused by decriminalization would increase the total amount of harm caused by both kinds of drugs. But this assumption is dubious. Decriminalization would allow consumers a much wider choice in the drugs they can take. There is no reason to believe that all (or even most) persons who otherwise would drink alcohol and smoke tobacco would do so if other options became legally available. Many users of these drugs would be expected to switch, and to curtail or even abandon their use of licit drugs altogether. As we know, alcohol and tobacco (along with caffeine) are the drugs most widely used for recreational purposes today. But we should not assume that these drugs would continue to occupy their predominant market position in the world of decriminalization. We simply do not know whether and to what extent users would substitute newly decriminalized drugs for those licit drugs they now tend to prefer. If a great deal of substitution took place, the enormous social harm presently caused by tobacco and alcohol might decline considerably. The total amount of harm caused by both categories of drugs might actually decrease.

Finally, the world of decriminalized drugs is hard to describe because it is not a monolithic world. I would anticipate that our fifty states would enact different regulatory schemes to respond to the problems caused by illicit drug use. Imagine fifty different rates of taxation, fifty different rules for compensating victims of harms caused by drug use, fifty different sets of laws governing production and sale, and thousands of different sets of rules and incentives created by corporations, schools, and insurance companies. The idea of a single blueprint for reform is at odds with allowing states to undertake experiments to determine what works best. Until these experiments are conducted, we should not be so foolish as to make confident predictions about how rates of drug use will change in a world of decriminalization.

In this section, I have provided several reasons to doubt that we have a clear idea about what the world would look like if illicit drug use were decriminalized. Too many unknown variables will affect the incidence of drug use when prohibition is repealed. How does this uncertainty affect our response to the basic question about criminalization? The answer is clear. Despite this uncertainty, there is *one* prediction about which we can be absolutely confident. In a world of decriminalization, those who use illicit drugs would not face arrest and prosecution. The lives of drug users would not be devastated by a state that is committed to imprisoning them. Punishment, we must always be reminded, is the worst thing a state can do to us. The single prediction we can safely make about a world of decriminalization is that it will dramatically improve the lives of the hundreds of thousands of people who otherwise would be punished for the crime of using drugs for recreational purposes. If our attitudes about decriminalization are shaped by our level of confidence in our predictions, we have excellent reasons to stop punishing drug users.

HARMS VERSUS BENEFITS

In this chapter I have described some of the positive effects of drug use, and provided a list of counterproductive effects of drug prohibition. Next, I offered several reasons to believe that we have no basis for confidence in our prediction about how illicit drug use, and the problems associated with it, would vary in a world of decriminalization. Still, I have no doubt that drug use causes substantial harm, both to individual users as well as to society in general. Does the bad outweigh the good? Is a world of decriminalized drugs *better* than a world in which people are punished for using (some) drugs for recreational purposes? Or would our world be a worse place if we stopped criminalizing illicit drug use?

One of the few points of agreement between many prohibitionists and their critics is that this is the fundamental question on which the fate of criminalization should depend. In other words, the common ground in the debate about prohibition is that *cost–benefit analysis* provides the framework in which our basic question should be resolved. Those who employ a cost–benefit analysis to assess our drug policy do not always use this terminology. They are more likely to use the term *harm-reduction*. This term, however, is somewhat misleading. No one really believes that an ideal drug policy should strive only to minimize harm. The point cannot simply be to reduce harm, but also to increase benefits. When properly understood, harm-reduction *is* cost–benefit analysis.

Why has cost–benefit analysis become so widely accepted as a methodology to evaluate drug policy? In the first place, the approach seems irresistible. In the words of Ethan Nadelmann, "who, in their right mind, could oppose the notion of reducing harm?"[44] But a deeper reason accounts for the popularity of cost–benefit analysis. As we saw in chapter 2, several thinkers purport to assess prohibition in *moral* terms. Some defenders of the status quo insist that illicit drug use is just plain wrong. Many of those who favor decriminalization, on the other hand, detect nothing immoral in recreational drug use. Where does the debate go from here? Moral disputes are notoriously intractable. Cost–benefit analysis offers a potential escape from this impasse. Those who apply a cost–benefit analysis tend to regard their methodology as different from and superior to a moral assessment. Their approach is empirical and scientific. We can use hard facts, not unsupported moral judgments, to evaluate our drug policy.

John Kaplan, a knowledgeable researcher on the pharmacological and social effects of drugs, expresses this point of view succinctly. According to Kaplan, the case for or against punishment "boils down to a careful weighing of the costs of criminalizing each drug against the public-health costs we would expect if that drug were to become legally available."[45] He is aware that "many people speak of the individual's right to do what he wishes with his own body, his right to harm himself, or his right to eat, drink, or otherwise ingest what he pleases." But he adds that "the problem with such 'rights' is that they are all assertions. They do not carry any argument with them." He continues, "perhaps . . . we would have a better and more moral society if we recognized [such 'rights'] as absolutes – but perhaps not."[46] Progress in the debate is possible only if we move beyond morality to a dispassionate weighing of costs and benefits.

Even though both sides in the debate tend to ask the same question, we should not be surprised that they provide diametrically opposed answers to it. According to Daniel Polsby, Associate Dean and Professor of Law at George Mason University, "the most serious, most sober argument for legalizing drugs . . . is not an argument rooted in principle but in practice. It is not that some grand moral precept confers a civil right on people to snort their brains out. The better argument is one of prudence rather than one of principle. Experience has shown that attempting to control people's drug consumption through the criminal law is far more costly than it is beneficial."[47] Gary Johnson, Governor of New Mexico, concurs. He writes: "A couple of things scream out as failing cost–benefit criteria. One is education. The other is the war on drugs."[48] But James Inciardi, Director of the Center for Drug and Alcohol Studies at the University of Delaware, arrives at a different conclusion. He warns that "the legalization of drugs could create behavioral and public health problems that would far outweigh the current consequences of drug prohibition."[49]

In this section, I will argue that both prohibitionists and their critics are mistaken about the single point to which they tend to agree. The fate of prohibition should *not* depend on a cost–benefit analysis. Instead, we must decide whether criminalization is just or unjust. Clearly, these perspectives are different. We have no reason to expect that arguments of justice will always support the same position we would reach by a cost–benefit analysis. A criminal law may be unjust even though it has more benefits than costs, or just even though it has fewer benefits than costs. When arguments of justice support different positions about our criminal laws than a cost–benefit analysis, we should retain those criminal laws that are just and reject those that produce more benefits than costs. Or so I will argue.

Let me begin by providing a very brief description of cost–benefit analysis. Anything we might want to evaluate – a law, an institution, or a policy – has advantages and disadvantages. Preparing a cost–benefit analysis is (deceptively) simple, and involves three distinct steps. The first step is to identify all of the possible alternatives to be evaluated. The next step is to list all of the benefits and all of the costs of each option. The final step is to weigh or balance each of the costs against each of the benefits. Supporters of this methodology contend that we should prefer and implement that alternative with the most favorable ratio of benefits to costs.

Why do I think that our basic question about criminalization should not be resolved in this way? In what follows, I will provide several different answers to this question. First, I will argue that we could not apply a cost–benefit analysis even if we tried. We do not have all of the facts we need. Even if we had all of the facts we need, we could not decide which alternative has the most favorable ratio of benefits to costs. Next, I will argue that cost–benefit analysis provides an inappropriate model for resolving our basic question about criminalization. Cost–benefit analysis is useful for resolving some controversies. But disputes about whether or not we should resort to the drastic step of punishment are not among the issues that cost–benefit analysis should resolve. Finally, I will challenge the motivation for adopting cost–benefit analysis. This methodology does not provide an empirical or scientific alternative to a moral assessment after all. A surprising consequence of my position is that the prediction that we have seen leads many prohibitionists to oppose decriminalization – fears about an escalation in illicit drug use – turns out not to be a good reason to inflict punishment, even if the prediction were accurate.

We can appreciate some (but not all) of the problems with a cost–benefit analysis by focusing on each of the three steps I have described. The first step should be relatively easy. I have assumed that we have two alternatives: Either we punish users of recreational drugs, or we do not. Obviously, this assumption is wildly oversimplified. We have a wide array of possible drug policies from which to choose. We might decide to punish users of some but not all illicit drugs. If we decide not to imprison users of a given illicit drug, we might decide to require them to undergo mandatory treatment. Nonetheless, I will pretend that we have only two alternatives to consider: decriminalization, and the prohibitionist status quo.

The second step, however, presents insuperable difficulties. We simply cannot begin to identify the costs and benefits of each of these two alternatives. Generating a list of costs and benefits might be possible for the prohibitionist status quo. After all, we should be able to describe the world in which we live. When these facts are gathered, our existing policy looks pretty bad. Even the most enthusiastic defenders of criminalization must admit that prohibition is counterproductive in many respects I have sought to describe. Moreover, our punitive policies appear to be largely ineffective. Nonetheless, prohibition almost certainly produces some benefits. Presumably, a list of all of these costs and benefits could be completed. But how can we possibly hope to identify all of the costs and benefits of the alternative I have tried to defend? In the previous section, I provided several reasons to doubt our ability to make accurate predictions about a world in which recreational drug use has been decriminalized. We cannot begin to identify the costs and benefits of a world about which we know so little.

Matters are further complicated by the fact that the anticipated costs and benefits of each alternative change rapidly. New technologies on the horizon may radically alter the current balance of costs to benefits. Consider, for example, the recent proposal to develop a killer fungus – a strain of *fusarium oxysporum* – that can be sprayed on fields of coca in Columbia. Some experts believe that this technology can kill much of the coca crop within a single year. For that matter, a similar fungus may be able to kill much of the world's supply of poppy and marijuana as well. Environmentalists caution that this plan may be too dangerous – some strains of *fusarium* kill virtually all cultivated plants, and could plunge the world into famine. Or the plan may be ineffective – coca producers might respond by developing new disease-resistant plants. But my point is not to decide whether this particular technological fix is realistic. My point is that such innovations may force us to revise our list of the costs and benefits of each option.

Suppose, however, that we somehow manage to solve the foregoing problem. We might improve the accuracy of our predictions about the world of decriminalized drugs. Imagine that we succeeded in producing a complete and up-to-date list of all of the costs and benefits of the two alternatives under consideration. How do we accomplish the third and final step? How can we possibly weigh or balance each of the costs and benefits against one another? The problem is that many of these costs and benefits are *incommensurable* – like apples and oranges. When a policy produces both good and bad effects – as is the case with any policy in the real world – we often lack a way to decide whether or not the positives outweigh the negatives. The metaphor of one set of reasons "outweighing" the other is misleading. When we use a real scale, we can easily decide whether one object is heavier than another. But reasons do not literally have weights that can be measured by precise instruments like scales. If costs are to be weighed against benefits, there must be some common denominator in which both can be expressed. What could this common denominator be? No answer is available in the present case. In the absence of a common denominator in which both costs and benefits can be expressed, we cannot complete the third and final step in the analysis. Reasonable people can agree about all of the costs and benefits of each option, but disagree about how these factors should be balanced. I see no empirical or scientific way to resolve their disagreement.

I am certainly inclined to believe that the costs of prohibition outweigh its benefits, and that decriminalization would produce the more favorable ratio. Obviously, my overall argument against criminalization would be strengthened if I could prove my belief to be correct. Unfortunately, I am at a loss to know how to persuade those who do not share my judgment about how to balance the costs and benefits of the two competing alternatives. Of course, my own ledger of costs and benefits differs radically from that prepared by prohibitionists. But the even greater problem is how to balance those costs and benefits that appear on both lists.

Perhaps the major obstacle in balancing the costs and benefits of these options is our inability to assign a weight to the most substantial benefit of recreational drug use: pleasure or euphoria. By definition, recreational activities are pursued for the sake of some positive psychological state. How much value does this psychological state have? If prohibition succeeds in accomplishing its objective of reducing use, how great a loss should we assign to the fact that persons who otherwise would have used drugs will be deterred from experiencing pleasure and euphoria? Alcohol, for example, is enjoyable, but causes hangovers and increases the risk of harms like automobile accidents. How on earth can we decide whether its benefits outweigh its costs? If our laws caused people to drink less, will this produce a more or a less favorable ratio of costs and benefits? We will be unable to answer this question unless we know how to weigh the enjoyment the drug produces. We will simply stare at the ledger of costs and benefits, unable to balance one against the other.

Of course, the foregoing problem is easy to solve if we assume that the euphoria of recreational drug use has *no* value. When prohibitionists prepare their list of costs and benefits, the central benefit of recreational drug use is conspicuous by its absence. The motivation to use drugs – at least, *illicit* drugs – is explained in terms of some pathology or human weakness that is not counted as a benefit. This exclusion makes the cost–benefit analysis relatively easy to complete. At the same time, the analysis becomes worthless. We are far more likely to believe that the benefits of prohibition exceed its costs if drug use *has* no benefits. Of course, recreational drug use *does* have benefits; I tried to describe them earlier in this chapter. But even though I am confident that these benefits exist, I have no idea how much weight to give them when they are balanced against the various costs of which prohibitions constantly remind us.

Nor can we possibly assign a weight to another major "cost" of prohibition. I have argued that criminalization is unjust, since no rationale in its favor is persuasive. Each purported justification for prohibition suffers from a common defect. They are overinclusive, allowing many drug users to be punished in order to prevent a harm that will be caused by only a small minority. Punishing people who do not risk whatever harm criminalization is designed to prevent is not simply a "cost" of prohibition. It is an injustice that should not be tolerated. In performing a cost–benefit analysis, how much weight should be assigned to this injustice? Obviously, principles of justice should not be ignored. But how can they possibly be included? As I suggested in chapter 1, justice functions as a constraint on what we otherwise would be permitted to do in trying to reach our objectives. To suppose that injustice is simply one additional factor to be placed on the cost–benefit scales is to misunderstand the nature and importance of justice. We should not implement policies that are unjust, even if they have favorable ratios of benefits to costs.

At this point, I should respond to a possible misunderstanding of my claims about the importance of justice. I have indicated that justice constrains or rules out alternatives that we otherwise might adopt in trying to reach an objective. Immanuel Kant believed that we are *never* permitted to commit an injustice. His view is extreme and unacceptable. Extraordinary circumstances might arise in which we *should* adopt an unjust alternative. We are permitted to commit an injustice if we need to do so in order to avoid a catastrophe. War, for example, may necessitate injustice. We should be prepared to tolerate the injustice of prohibition if it really were needed to avert a disaster. As we have seen, some prohibitionists use rhetoric to suggest that criminalization is needed to avoid a catastrophe that would take place if drug use were decriminalized. I have argued, however, that this rhetoric is grossly exaggerated, and that the reasons in favor of prohibition are not nearly good enough to justify our policy of punishing drug users. If my arguments are persuasive, I have also shown that the evils of drugs do not qualify as a catastrophe that should lead us to tolerate the injustice of prohibition.

Nor do I deny that cost–benefit analysis is possible and useful in many contexts. Suppose, for example, that we have a fixed amount of space in a public park. We have the resources to build a tennis court or a basketball court, but not both. What should we do? Presumably, such decisions should be based on our best efforts to identify the costs and benefits of each alternative. We should have relatively little difficulty in producing a list of these costs and benefits. Moreover, the costs and benefits of these options appear to be commensurable. In such cases, the application of a cost–benefit analysis seems both possible and appropriate. Cost–benefit analysis is *in*appropriate, however, in deciding whether to enact a criminal law. Even if my foregoing arguments are mistaken – and we *could* prepare cost–benefit analyses of prohibition and decriminalization – we should not allow our choice to be dictated by this methodology. I have suggested that criminal laws, by definition, subject offenders to punishment. When deciding whether to enact a criminal law, we are specifying the conduct for which offenders will be punished. In what follows, I will argue that our decisions about whether or not people should be punished, unlike our decisions about whether to build a tennis or basketball court, should not be made by applying a cost–benefit analysis.

It is absolutely crucial to appreciate why a cost–benefit analysis should not be used to decide whether to enact a criminal law. The reason is that criminal laws subject persons to punishment, and impositions of punishment are governed by principles of justice. To put the matter somewhat differently, punishment infringes *rights*. Decisions about whether we are justified to infringe a right should not be made by weighing costs and benefits. These claims require explanation. The first claim – that rights are infringed by punishment – is beyond controversy. I have defended this claim in chapter 1. When punishment is imposed, offenders are denied rights that we ordinarily take for granted. Clearly, we all have rights not to be tossed into a jail or prison, separated from our families and friends, and the like. The state infringes these rights when it punishes us. Because these rights are so precious, we need an excellent reason before the state is justified in doing these things to us. Justice requires that we may only be punished for compelling reasons.

The second claim – that cost–benefit analysis does not provide the good reason we need to justify infringing the rights denied by punishment – is slightly more controversial. Two different kinds of examples provide helpful evidence to support this claim. My first example involves an activity for which it seems probable that the costs outweigh the benefits, yet calls for prohibition would be absurd. The demand for punishment is ludicrous precisely because we recognize that cost–benefit analysis provides a poor rationale for criminalization. The second example involves a number of activities we all agree should be punished. Our confidence that criminalization is justified does not depend on the outcome of a cost–benefit analysis. We would continue to think that these activities should be punished even if we could be persuaded that the costs of criminalization outweigh the benefits. These examples help us to understand that we should not appeal to a cost–benefit analysis when called upon to justify punishing illicit drug users – even if such an analysis were possible to produce.

My first example imagines that we have prepared a cost–benefit analysis of television. Certainly a powerful case could be made that the costs of television exceed its benefits. Such a case has surprising parallels to the case against the use of recreational drugs. The following allegations have often been made, and are probably true. Television is bad for the welfare of our children. It desensitizes viewers to violence and thereby contributes to crime. It is deleterious to the health of those who watch more than a moderate amount of it. It undermines education by reducing reading and studying. Much of its content is morally objectionable. What are the countervailing benefits of television? Several advantages exist. Television conveys news and valuable information. Still, most people watch television for recreational purposes; television is immensely entertaining. I have no idea how to complete the final step in our cost–benefit analysis of television. The difficulties rival those of preparing a cost–benefit analysis of prohibition; we have no way to decide whether the recreational benefits outweigh the costs. But it is at least plausible to think that the costs of television would turn out to outweigh its benefits. Suppose (at least for the sake of argument) that this belief is correct. If so, why not criminalize the use of television, and punish those who watch it? Of course, the suggestion is preposterous. But what exactly is so outrageous about it? Why do we all know that a crime of watching television would be ludicrous? We know that we do not deserve to be punished for watching television, even if we agree that television fails a cost–benefit analysis. The kind of case I have sketched against television is not good enough to justify criminalization. I conclude that cost–benefit analysis does not provide a compelling rationale for punishment.

My second example involves activities that we all know should be punished, even though we do not rely on a cost–benefit analysis to defend the enactment of these criminal laws. No one maintains that we should punish murder, robbery or rape because the ratio of benefits to costs is more favorable for criminalization than for decriminalization. Someone may be uncertain about the outcome of a cost–benefit analysis of these crimes. After all, incommensurables are involved here as well. But this uncertainty is never used to raise doubts about whether these acts should continue to be punished. We would not be persuaded to decriminalize rape, for example, if we somehow discovered that the benefits of rape to rapists were far greater than we had previously believed. This discovery would be completely irrelevant to the case for prohibiting rape. We need not await the outcome of a cost–benefit analysis to know that these acts should be criminalized. We punish murderers, robbers and rapists because they deserve to be punished for their horrible and harmful acts. They deserve to be punished because they harm and violate important rights of their victims – not because their acts produce a net balance of costs to benefits.

Most of us are already aware that debates about criminal law and punishment should not be resolved by applying a cost–benefit methodology. Consider yet another example – the debate about capital punishment. How should we decide whether any criminals should be sentenced to death? We should not answer this question by trying to determine whether the costs of capital punishment outweigh its benefits. Those who argue about whether we save or lose money by executing criminals have missed the point. The death penalty should not be inflicted if it is unjust, even if its imposition produces more advantages than disadvantages.

Reasonable arguments about the justice or injustice of capital punishment can be made on both sides. But these are the kinds of arguments that need to be assessed if we want to use the appropriate framework to evaluate the death penalty.

These examples should persuade us that cost–benefit analysis, however insightful in other contexts, is not helpful in answering our basic question about criminalization. I belabor this conclusion because it supports a surprising and important consequence. The most significant benefit that many prohibitionists allege to justify criminalization – an anticipated reduction in the incidence of drug use – turns out not to be especially relevant to the case for punishment. In other words, anxieties about rates of drug use, even if well founded, do not provide a good reason for criminalization. This rationale fails on its own terms to answer our basic question of why we should punish people who use drugs for recreational purposes. The accuracy of such predictions is not really a very important factor in attempts to show that prohibition is just.

Does anyone really believe that individuals should be punished for something simply because the failure to do so would cause an increase in the behavior for which they are punished? This rationale fails to provide the *personal* justification for punishment that is needed. This is not our reason to criminalize acts like murder and rape. No one would say that we should punish these acts simply because the failure to do so would lead others to commit rape and murder. We can't be too confident whether these predictions are true. We might doubt that many people who presently abstain from rape and murder would be led to commit these crimes if they no longer feared arrest and prosecution. But this speculation is beside the point. We are justified in punishing rapists and murderers *regardless* of how punishment affects (or does not affect) the behavior of others. We would still be justified in punishing rapists and murderers, even if we were absolutely certain that the failure to do so would have no affect on the behavior of anyone else. We can reach the same conclusion if we return to my ludicrous example of criminalizing television. Someone who proposed to criminalize the act of watching television might point out that the failure to punish would be bound to lead to an increase in the behavior to be deterred. In this case, he is almost certainly correct. But he is just as obviously incorrect that this effect on behavior would provide a justification for punishment.

Perhaps we are tempted to believe that predictions about an increase in drug use (if accurate) are fatal to the case for decriminalization because we begin by asking the wrong question about drug policy. If we continue to focus on the right question – should drug use be criminalized? – I think we will be less likely to answer: "Yes, because drug use will increase unless we do." This latter answer does not begin to provide a personal justification for punishing drug users. It does not show that drug users deserve to be punished for what they have done. It is the kind of answer that might be given by the coach who is challenged to explain why he employs collective punishments, or the terrorist who is pressed about why he resorts to vicarious punishments. Predictions about how behavior would be affected by a change in our policy are less likely to persuade us to punish if we are careful to begin with the right question, and ask what justifies criminalization in the first place.

If criminal laws should not be assessed by cost–benefit analyses, how should they be evaluated? I have repeatedly insisted that our criminal laws must be just. Justice requires our criminal laws to be justified; we need a compelling rationale to resort to punishment. Cost–benefit analysis does not provide the compelling rationale we require.

As we have seen, however, even many of those who join me in opposing prohibition – like Daniel Polsby – reject arguments of justice in the cause of drug policy reform. Why are thinkers like Polsby so quick to dismiss the relevance of principles of justice in trying to resolve our basic question? I suspect that they, like their prohibitionist adversaries, neglect the importance of justice because they typically misidentify the nature of the principles at stake. Recall Polsby's derisive remark about the "grand moral precept" that "confers a civil right on people to snort their brains out." Of course, *this* is not the principle of justice at stake in the debate about prohibition. We must be on guard against a rhetorical trick that is often used in debates about criminal laws generally and prohibition in particular. Those who try to discredit arguments of principle on the side of decriminalization tend to formulate these principles very narrowly. No one can really believe that justice protects those who "snort their brains out."

Obviously, more general and abstract characterizations of the principle at stake add greatly to its plausibility. Perhaps justice protects us in deciding what substances to put into our bodies. Certainly, the latter principle is a good deal more attractive than the former, even if we ultimately reject both. At any rate, one grand moral precept *is* clearly at stake in the debate about prohibition. The only principle of justice we need to accept is that no one should be punished in the absence of compelling reasons to do so.

Those who favor decriminalization may be reluctant to talk about principles of justice for a different reason. John Kaplan has said such claims are "assertions" that "carry no argument." Why does he not make the same criticism of cost–benefit analysis? Recall the motivation for using a harm-reduction approach. Unlike moral argument, cost–benefit analysis is thought to be scientific and empirical. But this basis for preferring cost–benefit analysis is misguided. Critics of prohibition denigrate principles of justice at their peril, for a harm-reduction approach is no less dependent on moral evaluation than the alternative they reject. Cost–benefit analysis contains hidden moral evaluations at each of its three stages. At the first stage, we must decide which alternatives to consider, and which options should not even be entertained. We are unwilling to maim or torture drug users, for example, even if we thought that these draconian measures would make prohibition more effective. At the second stage, we must decide which consequences should count as costs, and which should be regarded as benefits. Moral evaluations are needed here as well. If pleasure qualifies as a benefit, for example, it is because pleasure is good. Finally, at the third stage, we must decide whether the costs exceed the benefits for each alternative. We could not hope to balance incommensurables unless we were willing to judge that some outcomes were more valuable than others. These judgments of value are moral judgments.

Cost–benefit analysis is dependent on moral evaluation in an even more obvious way. Our basic question about criminalization – should drug users be punished? – is a moral question. Nothing less than a moral reason can count as an answer to a moral question. We need a moral reason if we decide to prefer and implement that option with the most favorable ratio of benefits to costs. In other words, we need to reply to persons who demand to know why we should pay any attention to a cost–benefit analysis in resolving our basic question about criminalization. Only *moral* replies qualify as answers to moral "why should we ...?" questions. The only conceivable basis for preferring the option with the most favorable ratio of benefits to costs is that we have good moral reasons to do so. I have argued, however, that the better moral reasons entitle us to disregard cost–benefit arguments when trying to answer our basic question.

For the foregoing reasons, I am skeptical that we can or should use a cost–benefit analysis to decide whether to favor prohibition or its alternative. In chapter 1, I described how progress in the debate about drug policy was improbable if we begin by asking the wrong question. Progress is equally improbable if we employ the wrong methodology to evaluate our policy. We are far more likely to spin our wheels and reach no firm conclusions if we continue to speculate about costs and benefits than if we simply demand a rationale for punishing people who use drugs for recreational purposes – a justification for criminalization. I have little doubt that prohibition fails on cost–benefit grounds. If I am correct, principles of justice do not supply the only reason to prefer decriminalization. Still, I believe the better reason to oppose prohibition is because no good answer can be given to the basic question I have asked. If we lack a good reason to punish drug users, their punishment is unjust, and our punitive drug policies are unjustified. This is the *best* reason to favor decriminalization.

GETTING THERE

Suppose I am correct that drug prohibition is unjust – and almost certainly fails a cost–benefit test as well. People should not be punished simply for using illicit drugs for recreational purposes. Can our punitive policy be changed? Will it be changed? I have no blueprint for reform. My crystal ball is cloudy. As a legal philosopher, I have focused on arguments and principles, not on political strategies or forecasts. But the following observations provide some basis for hope. These brief remarks help to counter those pessimists (some describe themselves as realists) who share my conclusion but smugly predict that illicit drug use will never be decriminalized in the United States.

We should always remind ourselves how rapidly social transformations can take place. History is replete with examples of dramatic changes in legal policy that many experts believed could not occur. At the beginning of the twentieth century, few would have predicted that alcohol would be prohibited within a few years. Once enacted, however, most thought that prohibition was here to stay. In 1930, Senator Morris Sheppard, author of the senate resolution that later became the Eighteenth Amendment, confidently proclaimed: "There is as much chance of repealing the Eighteenth Amendment as there is for a humming-bird to fly to the planet Mars with the Washington Monument tied to its tail." Today, Sheppard is remembered more for his silly prediction than for his political achievements.

What must happen before any legal policy can be changed? Basically, two hurdles must be overcome. First, powerful and influential people must be convinced that existing policy is bad and that a better alternative exists. Second, they must be encouraged to act on their convictions, and to implement the option they believe to be preferable. In most cases, the first of these obstacles is greater than the second. In the case of prohibition, however, I am cautiously optimistic that this first hurdle can be surmounted, and that the second is the more formidable of the two.

I am confident that the first hurdle can be overcome after having made numerous efforts to persuade thoughtful people of the merits of decriminalization. On several occasions, I was prepared to provide a battery of reasons why our policy of selective prohibition should be changed. I was happily surprised to discover how many individuals already held this point of view. When academic conferences are convened to assess the pros and cons of our policy, it is surprisingly difficult to identify knowledgeable participants who can be relied upon to defend anything that remotely resembles the status quo. On the level of argument, much of the battle has already been won. Privately, many of those who have thought deeply about the issue agree that drug use for recreational purposes should not be punished.

My experience is equally favorable when I deal with non-academics who have not thought carefully about prohibition. In one-on-one dialogues, it is relatively easy to convince people of the merits of decriminalization. The case against criminalization appeals to individuals across the political spectrum – to conservatives and liberals alike. The more people bother to inform themselves about drug policy, the less likely they are to support it. Decriminalization is persuasive for the majority of those who are willing to invest the minimal time and effort to understand it. Of course, most of those who share my conclusion differ from me about the best reason to oppose prohibition. As I have indicated, criminalization is typically critiqued on cost–benefit (or harm-reduction) grounds. A survey by the Pew Research Center in March, 2001 found that 74 percent of the public agrees that America is losing the war on drugs. Popular films like "Traffic" fuel this attitude by portraying the futility of prohibition. The message is that the drug war cannot be won – not that its objectives are unjust. Prohibition is still thought to aim toward a noble goal – if only it could be made to succeed.

The particular reforms that have been adopted across the country reflect the popularity of a cost–benefit approach. Consider, for example, the growing movement to "treat, not punish." This movement has contributed to the proliferation of *drug courts* (sometimes called treatment courts, or drug treatment courts). Although the details differ considerably from one jurisdiction to another, the basic idea of a drug court is simple. Persons charged with minor drug offenses are diverted from ordinary criminal courts if prosecutors consent to bring charges in a drug court. Defendants agree to plead guilty and to accept placement in a drug treatment program. Court personnel supervise and monitor the progress of the defendant in the program to which he is assigned. If he completes his treatment regimen to the satisfaction of the court, his conviction is expunged. Failure to complete the program can result in incarceration – the punishment the defendant would have received if he had not agreed to treatment.

For the most part, the movement to "treat, not punish," has gathered momentum because of its favorable ratio of benefits to costs. It is not surprising, for example, that initiatives such as Proposition 36 originated in California. Our most populous state has the highest number of persons imprisoned for drug possession (19,000 in 2001), so sponsors of the Proposition were able to project that taxpayers could save 1.5 billion dollars in prison costs over five years. From a harm-reduction perspective, reforms that emphasize treatment are certainly preferable to massive incarceration. A 1997 study found treatment to be "7 times more effective than domestic law enforcement, 10 times more effective than interdiction, and 23 times more effective than attacking drugs at their source."[50] As a result of such favorable publicity, the number of drug courts across the country has grown to about 500 in 2001 from only twelve in 1994.

This reform, however preferable to incarceration, is a far cry from decriminalization as I have defined it. In the first place, the option of treatment is typically available only to first offenders. As I understand decriminalization, drug use would not be an offense at all, so it makes no sense to speak of drug users committing a second or a third offense. In addition, I believe this reform imposes a distinct and less severe mode of punishment, rather than an alternative to it. Why, then, be optimistic that this movement represents progress toward the goal I have defended? My answer is that mandatory drug treatment is bound to fail a cost–benefit test. At the present time, forced treatment may appear to be attractive on cost–benefit grounds. But just about *any* alternative to the status quo would achieve a more favorable ratio of benefits to costs. Coerced treatment is not cost-effective if we broaden the list of alternatives and include decriminalization among the viable options. The crux of the problem is that drug users need not have a condition that requires treatment. Why should we believe that people who seek euphoria or pleasure through the use of drugs must be suffering from a problem for which intervention is appropriate? How can treatment possibly be effective, when the mere act of drug use for recreational purposes – which provides the occasion to mandate treatment – does not qualify as a medical condition for which treatment is needed?

What *kinds* of programs will be mandated to treat the alleged disease of drug use? Treatment facilities are unable to accommodate the massive numbers of drug offenders who will be sent to them. Most existing facilities are twelve-step programs, which require persons to admit that they are powerless over their disease of addiction, and to invoke support from a higher power to help them become abstinent. We have good reason to be skeptical that these programs will survive a cost–benefit test. Why should we equate use with addiction, and suppose that even moderate recreational drug use amounts to abuse that necessitates intervention? The majority of users of any illicit drug are not addicts, but casual and intermittent users. What results would we anticipate if we made all drinkers of alcohol (and not just alcoholics) plead for spiritual support? No one pretends that all drinkers require treatment. What will we find when (literally) millions of arrestees are forced into these programs simply for smoking marijuana? Resistance from recreational drug users will be overwhelming. And why should we identify effectiveness with a lifetime of abstinence? Surprisingly, twelve-step programs have never been tested for effectiveness. No longitudinal studies show that these programs achieve better results than we find in a randomly selected control group of subjects who receive no treatment at all. Most illicit drug users stop taking drugs without formal treatment. We should not rely on anecdotes – testimonials of individuals who insist that they have profited from these kinds of treatment – to verify the success of twelve-step programs. Perhaps other kinds of treatments will emerge that produce more positive outcomes. At the present time, however, I believe that the same cost–benefit analysis that makes coerced treatment seem so clearly preferable to incarceration will reveal this option to be equally indefensible when compared to the costs and benefits of mandating nothing.

I suspect that many reformers who defend coerced treatment are aware of the problem I have described. Institutions like drug courts represent a compromise for those who reject our punitive policies but cannot quite bring themselves (either intellectually or politically) to require the criminal justice system to leave drug users alone. If I am correct to predict that the movement to "treat, not punish" will fail by the same criterion that made it popular in the first place, its primary achievement may be to help smooth the transition to decriminalization. It is hard to believe that the failure of this compromise will lead us to return to our policy of massive incarceration – the even more discredited alternative with which we began. Or so I hope. Admittedly, however, predictions about the future direction of drug policy are inherently fallible.

Other social forces may facilitate the implementation of decriminalization. One reason the United States is able to cling to expensive and ineffective policies is because it has enough money to do so. The wealthiest country on earth can afford the luxury of imprisoning people with little justification, or forcing them into treatment facilities with few prospects of success. If (or when) the next severe economic recession arrives, we will be more inclined to scrutinize these expensive policies on cost–benefit grounds. As a result, illicit drug prohibition may come to suffer the same fate as alcohol prohibition. Few living Americans remember the political controversy in 1932 about whether alcohol prohibition should be repealed. Shortly before the election, the Association Against the Prohibition Amendment (AAPA) published a pamphlet listing over thirty reasons to repeal the Eighteenth Amendment – most of which are equally applicable to illicit drug prohibition today. But Franklin Roosevelt saw no need to emphasize the injustice of alcohol policy. During the great depression, the economic arguments against prohibition were decisive in the minds of many voters. One wonders how long alcohol prohibition would have survived but for the monetary benefits of repeal.

At the same time, economic and political considerations militate against a change in our drug policy. We cannot fully understand the powerful hold of prohibition unless we appreciate who profits from it. Criminal justice officials and providers of drug treatment reap enormous gains from depicting recreational drug use as a grave social problem that our state cannot afford to neglect. The illicit drug user is alternatively portrayed as bad, and deserving punishment, or as sick, and needing treatment. My proposal to mandate *no* criminal justice response when persons use illicit drugs for recreational purposes will be bitterly opposed by those who profit from the status quo. They can be counted on to protect their economic interests by making pessimistic forecasts about the world of decriminalized drugs. Their efforts to frustrate fundamental reform will be aided by the political atmosphere in which criminal laws are enacted. New crimes are created – or punishments for existing crimes are increased – when a tragedy receives attention from the media. Drug abusers like Sue Miller are the topics of countless such stories. The injustice done to the many individuals I described in chapter 1 receive far less publicity. As long as policy about illicit drugs is shaped by anecdotes, the prospects for decriminalization seem bleak.

Where do our politicians really stand on drug policy? Consider the perspective of our highest elected officials. Whatever he may say publicly, it is hard to believe that President Bush really believes that people should be severely punished simply for using illicit drugs. During the campaign of 2000, he persistently responded to allegations about his past use of cocaine by describing his behavior as a "youthful indiscretion." His opponent, Al Gore, typically dismissed such matters as "private" and "no one's business." Both of these responses are correct, of course. Still, they cannot be reconciled with the belief that illicit drug users should continue to be punished. Can Bush or Gore really believe that they deserved to go to jail for what they (almost certainly) did? What else could it mean to describe behavior as "private" or as a mere "indiscretion" than that no one should be put in jail for it? After all, the drugs these candidates consumed apparently did not cause them irreparable harm. No one really thinks that justice would have been served had Bush or Gore been imprisoned for their conduct. These examples are hardly isolated. Indeed, persons who admit to having used illicit drugs have occupied both the White House and the Supreme Court well before 2000. I doubt that we will ever again live to see the election of a president who has not used an illicit drug at some time in his life.

The relative silence of candidates about drug policy during the presidential election of 2000 probably indicates that there is little political gain in anti-drug demagoguery. In previous recent elections, candidates were eager to outdo one another in promising an increasingly punitive response toward the "scourge of drugs." But the public does not automatically react favorably toward candidates who advocate further escalations in the drug war. Anti-drug rhetoric can no longer be counted on to win applause, especially in the black community. New York Representative Charles Rangel, who once advocated the deployment of military personnel and weapons in waging the drug war, now supports alternatives to incarceration for first-time drug offenders. Reverend Jesse Jackson openly denounces the "drug prohibition complex" that imprisons hundreds of thousands of minority youngsters. These leaders still oppose decriminalization as I have defined it. But hawks in our drug policy are becoming harder to find. Most news analysts were surprised when Attorney General John Ashcroft expressed his desire to escalate the drug war. Only a few years ago, such statements were commonplace.

Judges who are required to impose severe sentences on defendants convicted of nonviolent drug offenses are the most vocal opponents of prohibition in government. Judge Weinstein has characterized our drug policy as "utter futility." Judge Knapp has likened it to "taking minnows out of the pond." Judge Sweet demands that "the criminal prohibition against drug use and distribution be ended."[51] Another judge wondered whether in years to come he and his fellow jurists will have to plead the "Nuremberg Defense – I was only following orders" to justify the number of drug offenders they are sending to prison for decades.[52] Federal judges, of course, are lifetime appointees who need not fear that voters will retaliate in the next election.

One way to help persuade officials to be more courageous is to examine the fate of that handful of elected politicians who have dared to challenge existing drug policy. Kurt Schmoke, mayor of Baltimore, is one such example. Schmoke has long insisted that the drug war has caused more harm than good and that decriminalization should be seriously considered as a viable alternative. After making these controversial statements, Schmoke was re-elected twice. The most prominent politicians to question prohibition are Jesse Ventura, Governor of Minnesota, and Gary Johnson, Governor of New Mexico. Ventura openly acknowledges his history of drug use. Johnson is even more outspoken. He admits to having used considerable amounts of marijuana and cocaine in high school and college. He publicly proclaims that "our current policies on drugs are perhaps the biggest problem that this country has." He contends that "we are locking up nonviolent people senselessly" and "we ought to legalize marijuana. We need to stop 'getting tough' with drugs." How have these statements affected Johnson's political career? General Barry McCaffrey, the nation's drug czar, publicly condemned Johnson as "irresponsible" and "misguided." His chief law-enforcement official resigned in protest. A local sheriff called him an "idiot." His approval rating plummeted from 54 percent to 35 percent. Johnson himself, however, remained unfazed. Initially, he said that "politically, this [issue] is a zero ... For anybody who has a job associated with politics, this is *verboten*. I am on the ground, and the dirt is being thrown on top of my coffin ... This is the biggest head-in-the-sand issue that exists in this country today."[53] Later, however, Johnson claimed that phone calls became overwhelmingly supportive of his controversial stance. He maintains that a number of governors have told him privately that they respect him for what he has done, but that their careers would be over if they supported him in his cause.

But the above examples are exceptions; few politicians speak out. Publicly, most powerful and influential people retain a tough anti-drug posture, even when they privately sympathize with decriminalization. They often insist that their political fortunes and academic reputations require them to say something they do not really believe. They are confident that they would be ostracized for being "soft on drugs." Are they correct? Perhaps. But attitudes among politicians have come a long way in a relatively short period of time. An increasing number are willing to go on record as saying that our punitive drug policies are too severe. According to a recent survey, 80 percent of candidates for the New York legislature in the 2000 election favor abolition of the State's tough Rockefeller drug laws. Even sponsors of the original legislation concede that the laws have failed to deter drug use, and favor the restoration of judicial discretion when sentencing offenders who now are subject to mandatory minimums. Despite widespread dissatisfaction with these laws, the legislature consistently abandons plans to amend them. "Politics" is the reason why reforms with such levels of support are not actually implemented.

Since elected officials are reluctant to take the lead on this issue, we must look elsewhere for the impetus to change. The public may be ahead of politicians in embracing drug policy reform. But public opinion will not turn decisively against our punitive policies without counteracting the impression of illicit drug users as bad or sick. To change this image, some of the millions of users who have encountered few problems with illicit drugs must be prepared to "come out of the closet." Decriminalization will be a tough sell as long as the stereotypical drug user is perceived as evil, sick, pathetic, or decrepit. At the present time, voices of ordinary drug users are drowned out by tragic anecdotes like that of Sue Miller. At conferences and hearings, actual experience with drugs seems to be regarded as more of a liability than an asset – unless the user admits to having seen the error of his ways. Past experience is recognized as valuable in helping to shape the direction of policy only if the drug user has reformed. Nothing could erode public support for prohibition more quickly than a willingness among drug users to be more candid and unapologetic about their past and present behavior.

One encouraging trend (at least in this context) is the willingness of the Supreme Court to shift power toward the states and away from the Federal Government. This tendency may allow states to conduct experiments with less severe drug policies that would be unthinkable across the entire country. The various medical marijuana initiatives are evidence that many states are ahead of the Federal Government. Needle exchange programs to stem the spread of AIDS provide additional evidence. Prohibitionists will find it more difficult to argue that these programs have disastrous consequences when they are implemented without incident in states that are willing to take the lead.

Change is likely because the success of our existing policy is dependent on cooperation from the international community. Throughout the twentieth century, the United States persistently used its enormous influence to induce countries around the world to adopt a more punitive approach toward drug use. But foreign governments have grown increasingly dissatisfied by prohibition and have become much less inclined to enforce it. The United States is slowly losing its allies in the drug war. Little by little, countries throughout the world are daring to take new approaches. No western industrialized country is nearly as enthusiastic about criminalization as the United States. Majorities favor decriminalization in much of Western Europe, where punishments are far less severe. In England, public support for legalization of marijuana has risen from 26 percent in 1996 to 37 percent in 2001. Politicians are not far behind. A poll in 2001 indicated that 30 percent of Labour MPs favored decriminalizing marijuana immediately, without the need to hold further inquiries. In Canada, nearly half (47 percent) of all citizens favor allowing marijuana to be sold and used legally. Even some former Republics of the Soviet Union, long notorious for their tough anti-drug stance, have adopted far less punitive policies. In Ukraine, persons who possess drugs for personal use are no longer subject to arrest. Perhaps more importantly, drug-producing countries south of our border are openly skeptical of prohibition and the role they are asked to play in supporting it. The fundamental problem, from their point of view, is the insatiable demand for drugs in the United States. The case for decriminalization, compelling in the United States, makes even more sense in Latin American countries, which often depend on illicit drug production for their economic survival. Moreover, these countries seldom experience the problems associated with illicit drug consumption found in the United States. As we have seen, leaders in Uruguay and Mexico have recently had the courage to endorse decriminalization as a viable option. Jamaican Prime Minister Percival Patterson says he finds the arguments for decriminalizing the private use of ganja [marijuana] to be "persuasive." Of course, the United States reacts to these developments with threats of retaliation through "de-certification", which would mean the cessation of various aid packages for the failure to co-operate satisfactorily with the "war on drugs". In the case of some countries like Jamaica, de-certification would be politically destabilizing. Still, the United States cannot hope to stand alone in fighting a war against drugs when our neighbors and allies would prefer to declare a truce.

In conclusion, I want to express a modest hope that the legal philosopher can play a role in drug policy reform. As I have said, our society has little experience in conducting a debate about the wisdom of decriminalizing behavior that is punished at the present time. Socratic dialogue is the philosopher's remedy for confusion and uncertainty. When anecdotes are related about drugs and drug users, we must redirect the focus to the questions that need to be addressed – and clarify what will count as an acceptable answer to them. Most of those who become persuaded of the merits of decriminalization will probably arrive at this position on cost–benefit grounds. They will come to conclude that prohibition is ineffective and counterproductive. Everyone understands success and failure as measured in monetary terms. My contention, however, is that principles of justice provide an even better reason to reject prohibition. Economic arguments are made with such frequency because most people believe that disputes about justice are too complex and intractable. I have tried to counteract this mistaken impression.

If my argument required a comprehensive theory of justice, I too would be reluctant to base my case against criminalization on grounds of justice. Fortunately, my argument is noncommittal about the deep and controversial disputes about justice that have divided philosophers since the time of Plato. According to the minimal assumption I make here, justice demands that we have excellent reasons before we resort to criminalization. Punishment should not be invoked casually; it is a drastic step that infringes rights and liberties we all hold dear. Before we put people in jail, we had better be supremely confident that our policies are justified. No one, I trust, will contest this minimal assumption – even though they may disagree about other aspects of justice. In addition, I have made a claim that is only slightly more controversial. This claim involves the kind of reason that can justify punishment. I have supposed that a rationale for punishment must be personal. I mean that the reason that allows us to punish someone must be a reason that shows him to deserve punishment for something bad he has done. Justice does not allow someone to be punished because punishing him will somehow make the world a better place. I do not believe for a moment that the world is a better place because recreational drug users are punished. Still, controversial predictions about a world of decriminalization should be avoided if they cause us to lose sight of the fundamental principles of justice I have cited.

At the same time, I suspect that the main intellectual barrier to embracing decriminalization is not disagreement about the principles of justice I have mentioned, but confusion surrounding the facts about drugs and drug users. My case against prohibition applies relatively uncontroversial principles of justice to more debatable empirical claims about how drugs affect the people who use them. Many of these claims defy conventional wisdom. I have maintained that illicit drugs are not nearly as dangerous for adolescents as we are led to believe, that prohibition probably causes more crime than it prevents, and that illicit drugs are not especially unhealthy when compared to many recreational activities we would not think to punish. Prohibitionists are more likely to attack these empirical claims than to reject the principles of justice I have invoked. Who should we believe? I have mentioned the powerful economic incentives to retain prohibition among criminal justice officials and providers of drug treatment. When forming our opinions, we should ensure that our information is obtained from parties who lack a vested interest in preserving the status quo. When the facts are known, I am optimistic that we will conclude that our reasons to punish people who use illicit drugs for recreational purposes are not nearly good enough to justify criminalization. From a moral point of view, the case for decriminalization is compelling.

NOTES

1. Many of these anecdotes – as well as others – can be found in Mikki Norris, Chris Conrad, and Virginia Resner: *Shattered Lives* (El Cerrito, Cal.: Creative Xpressions, 2000).

2. David Hume: *A Treatise of Human Nature*, III.1.i.

3. Office of the National Drug Control Policy: *National Drug Control Strategy* (Washington, 1989), p. 11.

4. Office of the National Drug Control Policy: *National Drug Control Strategy* (Washington, 1989), p. 4.

5. John Morgan and Lynn Zimmer: *Marijuana Myths, Marijuana Facts* (New York: Lindesmith Center, 1997), p. 42.

6. Stanton Peele, Charles Bufe and Archie Brodsky: *Resisting 12-Step Coercion* (Tucson: Sharp Press, 2000), p. 29.

7. Office of the National Drug Control Policy: *National Drug Control Strategy* (Washington, 1990), p. 3.

8. Sourcebook of Criminal Justice Statistics, p. 232, Table 3.66 (2000).

9. See Arthur Trebach and Kevin Zeese, eds: *Drug Prohibition and the Conscience of Nations* (Washington: Drug Policy Foundation, 1990), p. 166.

10. Several longitudinal studies of drug users have been done. The best known is Jonathan Shedler and Jack Block: "Adolescent Drug Use and Psychological Health," 45 *American Psychologist* (1990), p. 612.

11. Deborah Frank, et al: "Cocaine and Pregnancy – Time to Look at the Evidence," 285 *Journal of the American Medical Association* (March 28 2001), p. 77.

12. See Paul Goldstein: "The Drugs/Violence Nexus: A Tripartite Conceptual Framework," 15 *Journal of Drug Issues* (1985), p. 493.

13. James Q. Wilson: "Drugs and Crime," in Michael Tonry and James Q. Wilson, eds: *Drugs and Crime* (Chicago: University of Chicago Press, 1990), p. 522.

14. William Bennett: "Should Drugs Be Legalized?" reprinted in Jeffrey A. Schaler, ed.: *Drugs: Should We Legalize, Decriminalize or Regulate?* (New York: Prometheus Books, 1998), p. 67 (emphasis in original).

15. *Ibid.*, p. 66.

16. *Harmelin v. Michigan*, 111 S.Ct. 2680 (1991).

17. See, for example, the evidence with respect to heavy, long-term marijuana use in Jamaica, Costa Rica and Greece in Lynn Zimmer and John Morgan: *op. cit.*, Note 5, pp. 8, 65, and 74.

18. Janet Joy, Stanley Watson, and John Benson, Division of Neuroscience and Behavioral Research, Institute of Medicine: *Marijuana and Medicine: Assessing the Science Base* (Washington D.C.: National Academy Press, 1999).

19. See, for example, Mark Kleiman and Aaron Saiger: "Drug Legalization: The Importance of Asking the Right Question," 18 *Hofstra Law Review* (1990), pp. 527, 545.

20. Shane Darke and Deborah Zador: "Fatal heroin 'Overdose': A Review," 91 *Addiction*. (1996), p. 1765.

21. Gail Winger, Frederick Hofmann, and James Woods: *A Handbook of Drug and Alcohol Abuse* (New York: Oxford University Press, 3rd. ed., 1992), p. 73.

22. Center on Addiction and Substance Abuse, Columbia University, The Cost of Substance Abuse to America's Health Care System, Report 1: Medicaid Hospital Costs, 1993.

23. Winger, Hofmann and Woods: *op. cit.* Note 21, p. 53.

24. *op.cit.* Note 14, p. 67.

25. Remarks by President Bush in announcing the new head of the Office of the National Drug Control Policy (May 10 2001).

26. See William Bennett, John Dilulio Jr., and John Walters: *Body Count* (New York: Simon & Schuster, 1996), pp.140 – 141.

27. See the 47 surveys described in Robert J. Blendon and John T. Young: "The Public and the War on Illicit Drugs," 279 *Journal of the American Medical Association* (March 18 1998), p. 827.

28. I borrow this term from Gary Johnson, Governor of New Mexico. See Gary Johnson: "It's Time to Legalize Drugs," in Timothy Lynch, ed.: *After Prohibition* (Washington DC: Cato Institute, 2000), pp. 13, 18.

29. James Q. Wilson: "Against the Legalization of Drugs," in James Inciardi and Karen McElrath, eds: *The American Drug Scene* (Los Angeles: Roxbury Pub. Co., 2nd ed., 1998), pp. 304, 311.

30. Andrew Weil: *The Natural Mind* (Boston: Houghton Mifflin Co., 2nd ed., 1983), p. 19.

31. Bennett: *op. cit.*, Note 14, p. 67.

32. See Jason Latrou, et al.: "Incidence of Adverse Drug Reactions in Hospitalized Patients," 279 *Journal of the American Medical Association* (1998), p. 1200.

33. For details, see http://www.fda.gov/ohrms/dockets/ac/00/minutes/3602m1.pdf.

34. See Howard Parker, Judith Aldridge, and Fiona Measham: *Illegal Leisure: The Normalization of Adolescent Recreational Drug Use* (London: Routledge, 1998), especially p. 89.

35. See David Musto: *The American Disease* (New York: Oxford University Press, 3rd ed., 1999).

36. See Jamie Fellner: "Punishment and Prejudice: Racial Disparities in the War on Drugs," 12:2 *Human Rights Watch* (May 2000).

37. *Op. cit.* Note 13.

38. J.H. Brown, et al.: "Students and Substances: Social Power in Drug Education," 19 *Educational Evaluation and Policy Analysis* (1997) p. 65.

39. Donna Haupt and Nancy Neary: "Justice Revealed," *Life* (September, 1987), p. 105.

40. James Q. Wilson: "Legalizing Drugs Makes Matters Worse," *Slate* (http://slate.msn.com/q/00-09-01/q.asp) (2000)

41. *Op. cit.* Note 14, p. 64.

42. *Op. cit.* Note 27.

43. Daniel Lungren: "Legalization Would Be a Mistake," in Lynch: *op. cit.* Note 28, pp. 179, 180–181.

44. Ethan Nadelmann. "Progressive Legalizers, Progressive Prohibitionists and the Reduction of Drug-Related Harm," in Nick Heather, Alex Wodak, Ethan Nadelmann, and Pat O'Hare, eds: *Psychoactive Drugs and Harm Reduction: From Faith to Science* (London: Whurr Publishers, 1993), p. 37.

45. John Kaplan: "Taking Drugs Seriously," 92 *The Public Interest* (1988) pp. 32, 37.

46. John Kaplan: *The Hardest Drug: Heroin and Public Policy* (Chicago: University of Chicago Press, 1983), p.103.

47. Daniel Polsby: "Legalization Is the Prudent Thing to Do," in Lynch: *op. cit.,* Note 28, p. 174.

48. Gary Johnson: "It's Time to Legalize Drugs," in Lynch, *ibid.*, p. 14.

49. James Inciardi: "Arguing Against Legalization," in his *Legalize It? Debating American Drug Policy* (Washington DC: American University Press, 1993).

50. Rydell, C.P., Caulkins, J.P., and Everingham, S.M.S.: *Enforcement or Treatment? Modeling the Relative Efficacy of Alternatives for Controlling Cocaine* (Santa Monica: RAND Corporation, 1997).

51. See Robert Sweet: "The War on Drugs is Lost," XLVIII *National Review* (February 12 1996), pp. 44–45.

52. Michael Isikoff and Tracy Thompson: "Hitting a Small Nail With a Very Large Hammer," *The Washington Post National Weekly Edition* (December 10–16 1990), p. 25.

53. *Op. cit.* Note 48, p. 19.

INDEX

INDEX

INDEX